Eat Slow Britain

Special places to eat, inspirational chefs,
gifted organic producers

Alastair Sawday

with Anna Colquhoun

Soil Association

Contents

Introduction

Alastair Sawday
Chairman of Alastair Sawday Publishing

The British are a curious people. We are very, very slow to adapt and change. We all know of our sloth in the face of German re-armament in the 1930s, of our refusal to re-arm even when faced with the most alarming threats. Then, once awoken, we responded with urgency and inventiveness.

We dug for victory. The nation gathered up its spades and grew its own vegetables with a new determination. Pigs and chickens strutted in a million back yards, every available piece of spare land became an allotment and the nation rediscovered its old, direct relationship with food. But it wasn't enough and we imported much of what we ate. After the war, chastened by our vulnerability, we drenched the land in newly-discovered chemicals in order to grow as much as possible. Old relationships were quickly forgotten in the headlong rush for productivity.

Now, with new global threats to our food supplies, will we once again respond with our spades, or will we continue to expect others far away to drench their land with those chemicals to produce food for us? The painful truth is that the chemicals are now seen to be toxic, the land and people are vulnerable, costs are soaring and international trade is fragile. So the far-sighted among us are turning back to that same land that responded so well to our digging. Here, at least, we can pay close attention to the food we grow and eat: its nutritional value, the way it is grown, the attitude of the farmer to wildlife and employment, the impact on the environment and – in the case of animals – the way they are kept.

Eat Slow is a celebration of the people who serve and produce our food with thoughtfulness. They are, I think, heroes of this new age of awareness, many of them putting the principle of good food first, and all of them driven by a profound understanding of the dangers we face if we don't sort out our food systems.

If you doubt that our food systems urgently need sorting, then do read Michael Pollan's *The Omnivore's Dilemma*, or Felicity Lawrence's *Not on the Label*, or *Fast Food Nation* by Eric Schlosser. Remember, too, the way the government quickly caved in to the lorry-drivers' strike a while ago. Look, too, at the average British High Street, wonder where the variety has gone and how few people control our food retail system. My own

> *"Eat Slow is a celebration of the people who serve and produce our food with thoughtfulness. They are, I think, heroes of this new age of awareness, many of them putting the principle of good food first and all of them driven by a profound understanding of the dangers we face if we don't sort out our food systems"*

community, Bristol, was cruelly divided by Tesco's recent bid to build a vast store in the heart of an area that has kept its small shops. It's all a bit of a mess, and the heroes in Eat Slow represent a way out of it.

Here are forty-five of our Special Places where you can eat very well and forty-three Soil Association-certified producers – all brought firmly under the Eat Slow banner. The stories range from rural loveliness to hard-hitting political work. There are doses of cynicism and of idealism. We have everything from cheese-makers to dairy farmers, veg box growers to cider-makers, chocolatiers, oyster gatherers and salami producers.

Some people we describe fit into neither category, such as Ashlyns Organic that has trained a network of school cooks and pulled together a co-op of Eastern Region farmers to supply them with fresh produce, Patrick Holden of the Soil Association and Guy Watson of Riverford. But they are heroes nonetheless, for they are, at cost to themselves, determined to promote the cause of good farming. They understand that the argument about organics so often misses the point: that when you buy the stuff you are buying a terrific package. You get good husbandry, animal and wildlife welfare, rural employment, freedom from toxic dangers, nutrition as good as any... and so on.

This remarkable book draws on the inspiration provided by a wide range of people and places. There are the pubs that are evolving into centres of the community, buying veg from customers, dealing direct with farmers and laying on cheap community lunches on pension-collection days. There are the Slow Food members organising food markets. There are the thousands of small, sometimes tiny, producers who barely scratch a living.

If you are worried about the cost of eating organic and the best local food, know that there are some great deals out there. During a recession, those who like to eat well will often do so at home, which is tough on restaurateurs. But the cutest among them are altering their dishes to keep prices stable, slow-cooking cheap cuts, making better use of vegetables. Poncy, overly-fussy food is rarer; provenance is more important than ever – and we are often told the story of the food we eat.

British farmers are still struggling to survive, with only patchy bits of good news. Those who sell direct to the public are doing better than most. One of the best stories to come out of the farming world in the last few years is the raising of nearly a million pounds for a young couple to buy the tenancy of Fordhall Farm. The many hundreds of investors believed in them. We need to become many millions – and invest in our own food supply.

Slow food need not be elitist. 'Good, clean and fair' is the motto of the Slow Food movement and we have followed suit by including the less expensive places to eat, the rustic places and those that can demonstrate that the best of food can be eaten by us all. I end with a quote from the owner of a pub restaurant in this book:

"Our suppliers eat and drink here too and so what better when a customer says the bacon he is eating is the best he has had in twenty years and we point him in the direction of the pig farmer sitting at the bar!"

Alastair Sawday

Introduction

Patrick Holden
Director of the Soil Association

The Soil Association's founder, Lady Eve Balfour, a woman wise beyond her time, thought that the key to good health was food produced 'not only from our own soil, but as near as possible to the sources of consumption'.

Eve Balfour was making a connection between people, place and food - a connection that has been a crucial part of our psyche for generations. Back in the 1940s, she was a brave pioneer swimming against the tide. The relationship between the people who produce our food and those who consume it was about to be eroded. When it finally disappeared, we also lost that link with the places where our food is produced; an almost spiritual connection between landscape and the enjoyment of its bounty. Eve was a woman with incredible foresight – something that I hope the Soil Association has continued. Yet who could then have foretold the damage that could be caused both to our own health and to the health of the environment by globalised and industrialised food systems?

This book celebrates a slow turning of the supertanker that is our food and farming system. It is not only a list of places where you can meet extraordinary food producers. It will connect you with a vibrant movement for change; people around the country who are challenging the orthodoxy of food production and building models that are both sustainable and rooted in their environment. In an age when global corporations have a frightening hold over people's relationship with food, this book celebrates food with a story. Each farmer, grower, retailer and chef listed here has a special relationship with the food he or she produces or sells. The stories in this book are inspiring and uplifting, yet they are but the tip of an iceberg. The Soil Association has a network of over four-thousand licensees around the UK, each one with a unique story and each one a food revolutionary – determined to change the way we think about food.

These new food pioneers – growers, producers and those who enjoy and value the fruits of their labours – know that change is coming. Rather like animals just ahead of a tsunami, they understand the urgency of the need to change the way we farm, produce and eat food. We are approaching a 'perfect storm' of climate change, resource depletion, diet-related ill health and population growth, all of which will force us to look again at how we produce and consume food. Our dependence on fossil fuel-derived inputs, global sourcing and centralised distribution is not sustainable. Neither does it allow us to be resilient against future shocks. Over the next twenty years almost everything about the way we farm, process, distribute, prepare and eat our food must be re-considered.

We are at a critical crossroads. The 'business as usual' option puts impossible pressures on resources, wildlife, landscapes and animal welfare; it causes the loss of small farms and farming jobs, it leads to unhealthy diets and the global spread of obesity and diabetes. The alternative is to balance our diets and turn to resource-efficient and environmentally-friendly farming methods – backed by the best scientific research into those methods.

In this book, you will get a flavour of what these new models might look like. The transition to a more sustainable food culture is not about giving anything up; far from it, it could vastly improve the quality of our lives - not least by reconnecting us with what we eat.

Food travels much further than it did thirty years ago; now it's time to slow it down. We have, short-sightedly, dismantled much of our regional food networks and infrastructure. Thousands of abattoirs, markets, butchers, bakers and greengrocers have disappeared as the food

"This book celebrates a slow turning of the supertanker that is our food and farming system. It is not only a list of places where you can meet extraordinary food producers. It will connect you with a vibrant movement for change"

system has become centralised. Over one-thousand local shops closed every week during the 1990s. Now we need to build a new system based on local networks. The food heroes in this book are testament to the fact that the tide is turning. Witness, for example, the increase in the number of community-owned shops. As their stories tell, they are not only producing wonderful food, they are developing new relationships with their communities; stronger bonds which are going to be crucial in an uncertain future.

How many of us know a farmer? In 1900, around forty per cent of the UK population was employed in agriculture; by the start of the Second World War that had fallen to fifteen per cent. Today it's less than two per cent. But when (rather than if) we switch to more sustainable farming methods like organic, many more people will be needed to work on the land; many new jobs will be created. Rob Hopkins of the Transition movement has called this 'The Great Re-skilling'. Farmers and growers will no longer be invisible; they will be among the most skilled and valuable people in the country. This book gives us some insight into who they might be – a fine way of getting to know more of those food producers on our doorstep.

I hope this book uplifts you as it does us. At the Soil Association we are working alongside communities around the UK to prove that change is possible. Please look at our website to find out how to join us – and what role you can play in this food revolution. Issues like climate change and peak oil can sometimes make us feel powerless; but food is different. Wendell Berry, the philosophical farmer and writer, described eating as an 'agriculture act' and he is right. We can all take action to change our relationship with food, with the countryside that sustains us, with the people who make it what it is. We can do it every day, three times a day.

Patrick Holden

South, Central & East England and Wales

Key

● Alastair Sawday's Special Places to eat
● Soil Association certified organic producers

Map 1

North England and Scotland

Key

Alastair Sawday's Special Places to eat
Soil Association certified organic producers

Map 2

The Slow Food movement

No wonder the Slow Food movement was born in Italy. It's less of a country than a collection of regions, each with a strong sense of its own cultural and food heritage. Each boasts its own shape of pasta and fresh produce that it claims as its own. It's a country where Sunday lunches are multi-generational family feasts lasting long into the afternoon. The exact birthplace was the Piedmontese town of Bra, in an area famous for its wines, cheeses, beef and truffles.

During the eighties a group of young people, headed by Carlo Petrini, became concerned about changes in their country's food culture. Traditional and regionally distinctive foods were being lost to standardised restaurant menus, industrialised food production and supermarket dominance. Connections between consumers and producers, and between food and culture, history and geography were being eroded. Food was consumed for fuel, not for pleasure.

Two events hardened Petrini's resolve: the opening of a McDonald's in the heart of Rome and the poisoning of hundreds of people by wine cut with methanol. Italian food was in crisis, and the story was similar elsewhere. In 1989, delegates from fifteen countries signed the Slow Food Manifesto: "In the name of productivity, Fast Life has changed our way of being and threatens our environment and our landscapes. So Slow Food is now the only truly progressive answer."

Today, Slow Food has over one-hundred-thousand members in one-hundred-and-thirty-two countries. American vice-president Alice Waters says, "fast food is a dead end: besides being damaging to our health and environment, it has changed our culture. Fast food makes us think everything in life should be fast, cheap and easy."

Instead, Slow Food champions food that is "good, clean and fair", supports food that is natural, fresh and flavoursome and produced without harming the environment, animal welfare or human health. It also demands that there should be fair pay and conditions for all involved.

Local Slow Food groups organise sociable tastings of artisan foods and a chance to meet producers. There are initiatives to improve hospital and school meals and create edible school gardens. And large food fairs, such as the biennial Salone del Gusto in Turin, bring together thousands of producers, cooks and food-lovers.

By discovering the stories behind the food on our plates, we share responsibility for how it was produced and, the fact that our shopping choices affect others, makes us partners in production.

Slow Food has also created an 'Ark of Taste' detailing hundreds of threatened small-scale artisanal foods: cured mullet roe made by women's groups in Mauritania, a smoked Polish mountain sheep's cheese called oscypek, the ancient breed of Norwegian Villsau sheep, four colourful varieties of Peruvian sweet potatoes, traditional perry of the Three Counties and Welsh Marches.

But this is not about preserving the past in aspic. 'Presidium' projects provide practical support, helping producers develop their product and expand their market, to the benefit of the rural economy. Through Slow Food's unique Terra Madre network, thousands of growers, herdsmen, fisherfolk, winemakers, cheese-makers and other artisans unite to share their experiences.

Petrini realised a new generation of gastronomes was needed – people who understood the complex economic, political, agricultural, ecological and social dimensions to food, as well as the culinary and the nutritional. In 2004, he opened the University of Gastronomic Sciences.

A wider Slow movement has emerged that seeks quality in all aspects of life: work, travel, sport, finance, education, architecture. Internationally there are now over one hundred and twenty towns in the Cittaslow network, including Ludlow, Mold and Perth in Britain, which foster local distinctiveness and community spirit.

As Slow proponent Carl Honoré says: "Slow is about doing everything as well as possible, instead of as fast as possible". The diverse food businesses in this book are united by this simple approach.

Slow Food International
Piazza XX Settembre, 5
12042 Bra (Cuneo), Italy
T: +39 0172 419611
E: international@slowfood.com
www.slowfood.com

Slow Food UK
6 Neal's Yard, Covent Garden
London WC2H 9DP
T: 020 7099 1132
E: info@slowfood.org.uk
www.slowfood.org.uk

South England

Key

Alastair Sawday's Special Places to eat

Soil Association certified organic producers

Map 3

South England

The Gurnard's Head

Zennor St Ives
Cornwall TR26 3DE
01736 796928 www.gurnardshead.co.uk

Rustic and full-flavoured, the food here would appeal to Elizabeth David. It is modelled on what people might cook at home, or at least used to, and professionally rendered by chefs with Michelin-starred backgrounds. "'Simple things done well' is our mantra," says Charles Inkin who, with brother Edmund, also owns the Felin Fach Griffin in Brecon (see page 178).

The old coaching inn stands alone a short walk through the grazing fields from the restless Atlantic on the dramatic coastline between St Ives and Penzance. It's a well-known landmark, its Georgian ochre walls contrasting vividly with windswept moorland.

Head chef Robert Wright's menu is short, homely and seasonal. Winter brings ham bubble and squeak with

The large garden has seascape views and afternoon barbecues, weather-permitting. It draws the crowds and Charles recommends the sleeper train from London for the most relaxing way to arrive in the area and will pack you a picnic for the Sunday night return journey.

Spring and autumn bring coastal path walkers who are grateful for the Gurnard's Head's rich fish soup, homemade terrines and hearty stews. Winter is quieter, with just locals left to brave the weather for a reward of homemade fruit cake and mulled apple juice spiked with Somerset cider brandy in front of the fire.

"Appealing to both tourists and locals could be difficult, but this spot is so wild and magical that it is a magnet," says Charles, who keeps local ales and ciders on

a fried egg, lamb with haricot bean purée and spicy harissa, and wholesome beef and barley broth. In summer simply cooked seafood is served: grey mullet with new potatoes and aïoli, gurnard with spinach and salsa verde, hake with pancetta and peas. Desserts lean towards the nursery: gooseberry fool, lemon posset, Eton mess and bread and butter pudding.

tap, local art on the walls and a local address book for suppliers and tradesmen. On Monday nights two regulars play old Cornish folk songs to a small but committed crowd. "It keeps alive a local tradition that's almost extinct," says Charles.

Charles was himself a chef and trained at Darina Allen's inspirational Ballymaloe cooking school in Ireland.

"They were doing the 'local' thing years before it was trendy – chefs who train in cities miss that whole connection with the land. Cooking has become driven by convenience, in homes and restaurants, so people are buying semi-prepared foods and ignoring the food producers that live close to them."

Soon after opening, Charles placed a sign outside saying 'we want your fruit and veg'. Gardeners, smallholders and farmers responded enthusiastically. Meat comes from a traditional butcher and grazier in St Ives, herbs and edible flowers from Keigwin Organic Growers, venison from local gamekeepers, and drinks and yogurts from Plough to Plate, who specialise in Cornish produce. "The Cornish Duck Company's birds are the

Alexanders – similar to celery – with mousseron mushrooms and pecorino, or nettle soup with crème fraîche. And look out for the dates of Caroline's gourmet foraging classes to discover the unsung potential of elderberries, wild fennel and jelly ear fungus.

For overnight guests, winter breakfast is taken in front of the fireplace and in summer around an old baker's table which seats fourteen.

"I love communal dining," says Charles, who encourages private parties to order boards of nibbles and giant pots of stew to share. "People discuss the best local walks over their scrambled eggs, and some end up hooking up for supper too. It's much more natural and friendly to share a table and eat together."

happiest I've seen and the tastiest I've eaten," says Charles. "Small Cornish food producers are in a precarious position and are being hit hard by the recession. But we'll stick by them."

Caroline Davey, a professional ecologist and forager, drops by weekly with edible wild greens – sorrel, sea purslane, sea spinach, rock samphire. In spring try

The Gurnard's Head

Evening main courses £11.50–£16.50
Best meal deal: Sunday lunch, £12.50
Food always available
Nearest train: Penzance

Baker Tom

Truro Cornwall TR15 3SF
08453 884389
www.bakertom.co.uk

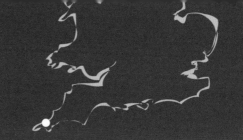

"I never thought I'd be a baker," says twenty-five-year old Tom Hazzledine. "I was one year off completing a degree in Computer Technology when I took a summer job at a farm shop in Cornwall. When they lost their supplier of bread, I stepped in with my own homemade stuff." Tom cycled in to work with his four loaves, which soon doubled to eight, then more, as customers snapped them up. Within weeks Tom had given up on his degree and had his own bakery. Every few months since he's moved to larger premises as demand has surged. In 2007 he opened a shop in Truro and plans to open another.

It's a tough job and the hours are antisocial. While his peers are in the pub, Tom is rolling pastry, shaping loaves and loading up the ovens. All night long. After packing the delivery vans before breakfast, he dusts off the flour and turns his attention to the paperwork, finally heading home to sleep in the early afternoon, returning at ten.

Tom bakes over two hundred loaves a day and has a legion of fans. He loves baking and doesn't mind the hours. "I could never go back to university or work for someone else. I just love seeing the raw ingredients of flour, water, salt and yeast transform into bread. And it smells so good!" It was the visit of an Indian woman to Rosebery Primary School in Loughborough in 1990 which launched Tom's love affair with dough at the age of six.

"She talked about chapattis and my brother and I wanted to try making our own, so we mixed up flour and water in the bathroom sink and then tried to bake it in the oven. We made a hell of a mess."

Though Tom's father was a baker and has run several restaurants, Tom is largely self-taught and masterminds a complicated production schedule of up to twenty-five different breads at any one time. "The focaccia flies out the door, as does our carrot, mustard and thyme bloomer. And our Guinness and black treacle bread won the 2008 Royal Cornwall Show best new product award." Tom favours seasonal ingredients and small local producers. "I wouldn't want to use a large, anonymous supplier. Being part of the local food network is very important to me." His hero is the renowned artisan baker Dan Lepard who has worked with many chefs including Giorgio Locatelli.

Customers include kids popping in for sweet treats after school, staunch regulars who come from Plymouth on the train each week, smart restaurants in Truro and Falmouth and hip beach bars catering to the surfing crowd. Jamie Oliver's Fifteen at Watergate Bay now stocks his bread too. "There's even a man who comes from Yorkshire every month to stock up for his local restaurant and friends, and a six-year-old girl that we make special loaves for because she can't eat dairy or wheat."

Tom believes that industrially made bread may be behind many of today's wheat intolerances. "For a start there's the crust," he explains, "Supermarket bread has no real crust, so you don't chew it properly. Chewing triggers the enzymes needed to fully break down the bread in our stomachs. But you get what you pay for, and for £2 you

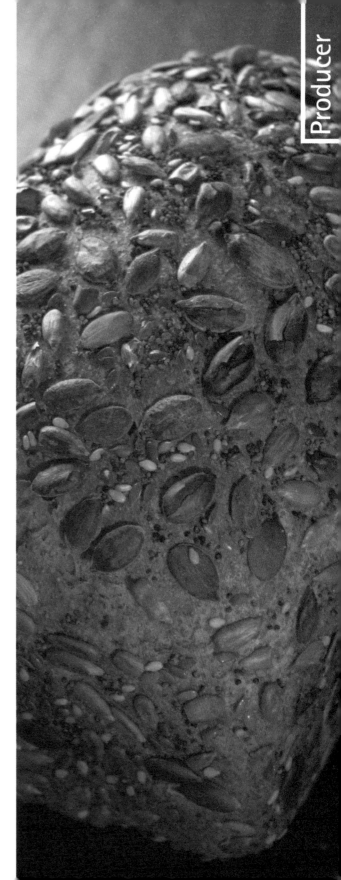

can have a good quality loaf without all those enzymes, conditioners and anti-fungal sprays. I want to reassure my customers I'm using the finest ingredients, which is why we're certified organic."

The eleven organic flours he uses are from Shipton Mill in Gloucestershire where the presence of a mill there was recorded in the Domesday Book. Shipton promotes old and rare grains and some flours, like the wholewheat, are stoneground, just as they would have been in medieval times, to retain more of the grain's natural goodness. The yeast is not organic as Tom hasn't found a reliable supplier, but is always fresh and never made from genetically-modified products. In place of large doses of baker's yeast, Tom prefers to use their natural sourdough starter ("the bakery's baby") and plenty of time. While industrially made loaves can be done in thirty minutes, most at Baker Tom take at least five hours, with the one-hundred per cent sourdough needing around twenty-four, depending on the weather.

The 'Slow' approach continues at the baking stage. During the summer staff fire up their custom-built brick oven. "Baking in that really is going back to basics," says Tom, "You can't get any better than starting with a fire. With conventional ovens it's all about exact timings and temperatures, but with this you have to understand all its hot and cold spots, which change every day. The woods and herbs we use each give different smoky flavours."

Somehow amid all this, there is also time to run masterclasses. "I'll help people produce better bread using their own oven and things they've probably got lying around already, like water sprays to create steam, garden tiles as pizza stones and terracotta pots instead of tins. Bread should be like other food: you regularly make it at home yourself and then get it from a restaurant or bakery when you don't have time or fancy something special."

Tom is full of infectious enthusiasm and ambition. He has more ideas than time but every now and then when he's not elbow-deep in dough he launches another. The delivery vans will run on biodiesel; soon their bread will appear in local box schemes. "I have a mentor, an older guy who's a solicitor, who tries to keep my feet on the ground and steer me in the right direction. But sometimes I just jump in and do it anyway."

Lansallos Barton Farm

Lanteglos by Fowey
Cornwall PL23 1NH
01726 870375

When the National Trust agreed to Mark and Charlotte Russell taking over Churchtown Farm in 1992, it was the first time they had accepted a business plan based on organic farming. "It wasn't easy to convince them. They thought it would be messy and weedy," recalls Charlotte. The National Trust soon realised the young couple were serious beef and lamb farmers with a mission to restore this run-down stretch of Cornish coastline. "I think they're pretty proud of the farm now," says Charlotte. "They have now let many more farms to organic tenants, so things have changed."

In the '70s and '80s pressure on farmers to increase yields resulted in intensive mono-cropping. There was no rotation system in place and the hedges were in disrepair and that took its toll on soil fertility, wildlife and coastal vegetation. The Russells don't blame their predecessors: "farmers were caught in a vicious spiral of having to produce more and more". Today six-hundred-and-eighty-acre Churchtown Farm, which includes nearby Lansallos Barton Farm, is one of the largest and most important areas of conservation in Cornwall.

As a reporter for Farmers' Weekly, Charlotte concluded the organic approach was, simply, "right". She met Mark while filming a documentary; he had taken time out from the conventional arable family farm in Wiltshire to learn from organic farmers. "We'd both been inspired by early farmers in the organic movement who were powerful thinkers and their ideas on sustainability and environmental principles made sense."

Almost two decades after Mark and Charlotte started farming organically the man-made distinction between farmland and wild cliff edge has faded away: barn owls and skylarks have returned and fertile grasslands provide

a rich diet of clover and herbs for the cattle and sheep. Mark never needs to buy feed.

"We manage the land as one unit," explains Charlotte, "so farm melds into coastal fringe." The

South Devon, Ruby Red and Aberdeen Angus cattle and Welsh Lleyn sheep were chosen to suit the naturally grassy cliff-top topography. The Russells see eating meat as a logical part of the ecological cycle: "The animals utilise the grass and manage the landscape that is so dear to many people."

The Russells' meat – made so delicious by the varied grass diet and longer hanging time – has attracted awards. "Ours is a completely different colour from supermarket beef, it is much darker red and it tastes so different." Unusually, lambing starts in May, in line with nature's cycle when the grass is growing. "Other farms lamb in winter to hit the Easter market when prices are high," explains Charlotte, "but this means ewes are inside, there's more chance of disease and you need to buy extra feed." The Russells' prices reflect their slower and less intensive rearing, and they find their customers, who insist on top quality, pay the price and eat less.

Small amounts of lamb and beef are sold through the farm, but the majority is sold through Ben Watson's Riverford Farm shops and meat boxes (see page 30). "We can supply Riverford all year, at an agreed, fair price, and they take all we have. We never let each other down. When you deal with supermarkets you never know how long your relationship will last or how they will change the price. It's less fair and it's scary."

The business is low key: Lansallos has no website, marketing person or necessary farm shop. They are hidden away behind the coastline, like the pirates who used to smuggle in tea, gin and tobacco in the eighteenth century. In summer they open a tiny tearoom for cream teas and a small National Trust campsite overlooking the sea. The coastpath dips down to pristine, secluded coves one way and up past the grazing sheep and the thirteenth-century fishing village of Polperro the other.

"Cornwall is popular with second homers and holidaymakers but it's a very poor county," says Charlotte. "Many who work for the minimum wage or below can't afford the food that is produced here." The Russells make a point of employing local people and using local services and suppliers; they host groups of schoolchildren, too. "We want to get the next generation thinking about food and its provenance. That's the most important work we do."

"*Ours is a completely different colour from supermarket beef, it is much darker red and it tastes so different*"

The Harris Arms

Portgate Lewdown
Devon EX20 4PZ
01566 783331 www.theharrisarms.co.uk

"If a small country pub is to survive it needs a hands-on approach, a reputation for its food and good, friendly service," says Andy Whiteman, owner of The Harris Arms. "We make a point of greeting customers when they arrive and saying goodbye when they leave, it makes a big difference."

The Harris Arms, formerly two sixteenth-century cob cottages, is perched on the Cornwall-Devon border with eye-stretching views. People primarily come to eat and it's a convenient stopping-off point on the A30 that speeds people through the West Country. The cooking is robust and confident, using fresh ingredients and, as much as possible, local produce. Starters include roast breast of pigeon with beetroot risotto, local goat's

have had regular entries in the Michelin Guides.

The biggest surprise at The Harris Arms is the wine list: over one-hundred bottles, all extremely well-priced. Andy and Rowena trained as winemakers in New Zealand and lived and worked with winemakers in France for a year and a half. They brought their knowledge back with them to the UK and have built an award-winning wine list.

"We import fifteen to twenty per cent ourselves from small vineyards or from ecologically-sound larger ones, and use around twenty merchants," says Andy, who wants people to experiment with wine without spending a fortune. "We put on a cash mark-up, rather than work on gross profit margins. We sell a £24 bottle

cheese on croutons with pesto and dressed leaves and the very popular prawns Piri Piri. Mains vary from slow-cooked pork belly with a unique twist on potato and black pudding croquettes to pub classics such as fish and chips.

Since Andy and Rowena Whiteman bought the pub in 2003, they have won many awards including Newcomer of the Year in 2003, Licencees of the Year in 2006 and

of wine that, elsewhere, would be £40. The more money people spend on wine here, the better value they get!" This extends to the food. The practice of buying local produce means that they provide good value, support local businesses as well as reducing their carbon footprint. "We work out fair deals with our suppliers, buying game, beef, venison, pork, lamb from local farms and businesses."

detract attention from questions around the bulk of our consumption. Indeed, he says, many shoppers will enjoy the warm glow of buying Kent apples over South African, then pop a pineapple in their basket.

Guy bases his environment decisions on two years' research with Exeter University. "What counts is how things are grown and transported. Take tomatoes: those grown in the natural heat of Spain have a lesser environmental impact than British ones grown in heated greenhouses." The research also revealed that vegetables shipped from western France create a fifth of the emissions of those trucked from Spain. So Guy acquired a farm in the Vendée within striking distance of a port, where the sunny climate nurtures a good range of vegetables over a long growing season, filling Britain's 'hungry gap' in April and May.

Although always suspicious of chemical sprays, Guy admits he switched to organic farming largely for commercial reasons. "It took me several years to get into the whole philosophy. You need a conversion period – it's about cleansing your head as well as the soil."

But people kept challenging him: can organic farming feed the world? He hoped to find the answer in Africa. In Uganda, Kenya and Togo Guy was depressed by how little benefit exports brought farmers. "Any profit is usually pocketed by Western middlemen. And growers are at the mercy of European supermarket buyers, who might source their organic Fairtrade pineapples from Togo one day and then from Costa Rica the next, depending on the exchange rate.

"Without any doubt the world has a better chance of feeding itself through organic agriculture. When oil runs out, it won't be a problem for African growers as they're farming without it already. Better agricultural training and longer-term trade agreements are needed, too."

Guy's world resembles a jigsaw. He loves piecing together an idea worth more than the sum of its parts. "We want to connect people to their food and have a bit of fun," he says. He's planning a cookery school for school-leavers and has set up classes with Riverford Cooks to help customers use up their veg boxes.

Also in the pipeline are plans for a travelling pop-up restaurant in a yurt...

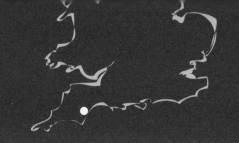

Occombe Farm

Paignton Devon TQ3 1RN
01803 520022
www.occombe.org.uk

Occombe Farm was destined to become a golf course but vigorous local campaigning saw the land designated as a Site of Special Scientific Interest. Tenant farmers had never worked the land intensively or made dramatic changes for they never believed it would be theirs for long. Ironically, it was the threat of development that preserved the land.

The organic farm is run by the Torbay Coast and Countryside Trust and has an award-winning café, shop, bakery and butchery. "Our aim is to reconnect people with food, farming and the countryside," says Julian Carnell who is the Educational Manager for the Trust. "If we are going to engage people in issues such as climate change and peak oil we need to do it in an accessible way. Local food is a great place to start."

Heavenly aromas drift from Rob Hooley's artisan bakery into the all-day café upstairs. Rob's loaves, baps and cakes, baked daily, are made with organic flours from Shipton Mill. Local cheeses, fruit and vegetables, pasties, ciders and wines line the shop's shelves.

Rainwater flushes the loos and a wind turbine and solar panels provide power. The education centre and teaching kitchen was constructed out of old car tyres, straw bales and home-grown timber by students from a local college. Here, you can learn to bake bread, make cheese, preserve hedgerow berries and weave baskets. Children use computers to calculate food miles on the beef, tomatoes and bananas in the shop and at the weekly cooking club youngsters grind wheat for their bread.

"We hope that if they learn what goes into making cheese, or bread, in the future they'll think twice about what they buy," says Julian. The activities are hands-on, so participants create their own lasting sight, sound, touch and taste memories. "We show people how their choices are connected to the environment, animal welfare, the economy and their health and when buying meat, for example, we should consider what's behind the price-tag.

"Every town can tell a story about disconnection with food," says Julian. His parents remember the traditional butchers, Foale's Corner, in Paignton that was supplied by Lawrence Foale's own farm. Today, it is a Tesco Metro. Julian is proud that Occombe provides an alternative to supermarkets.

A nature trail weaves through the woodland – Occombe means 'oak valley' – and wildflower meadows, past the Oxford Sandy and Black pigs and Dorset Down sheep, via the bird hide and back to the orchard.

"Twenty breeds of British farm animals became extinct in the twentieth century. Preserving rare breeds is essential to maintain the genetic pool," explains Julian.

Schoolchildren are busy about the place, identifying species in the dense hedgerows, counting spiders, crafting nest boxes, feeding animals and collecting eggs from the Light Sussex hens. For many, it's their first time on a farm. "They turn up in smart white trainers, not expecting mud and mess as often their only food experience has been in a supermarket where everything is in sanitised packets."

Occombe is open to visitors, free of charge, every day. Subsidies from the Trust and grants keep classes reasonably priced. A Community Supported Agriculture project has started where participants will tend and harvest vegetables, and then follow them from field to plate in the straw-bale community kitchen. The project will create some volunteering and training opportunities for ex-offenders, too. If successful, Julian hopes to replicate the model on pockets of land close to Torbay's most deprived housing estates. "Local, organic food should not be a niche market," he insists.

There's a beer festival in June and pumpkin-carving parties in October. Or come to learn old skills such as water dowsing, apple pressing, hedge laying and mushroom hunting. "Occombe is not stuck in times gone by," assures Julian. "We learn from the past, preserve the best bits, and reinvent them for the future."

"If we are going to engage people in issues such as climate change and peak oil we need to do it in an accessible way. Local food is a great place to start"

Rod and Ben's

Bickham Farm Ken Exeter
Devon EX6 7XL
01392 833833 www.rodandbens.com

"You can debate the nutrition levels of organic food but you can't question my taste buds. I know it tastes better," says Rod Hall. "One of the great benefits of farming how we do is getting to eat some of the best food available." You can't help but envy him – a man who can barbecue his own pedigree Dexter beef steaks and pick an impressive range of vegetables straight from the soil.

Bickham Farm's one-hundred-and-six undulating acres near Exeter are also home to rare Devon and Cornwall Longwool sheep, hens, honeybees and a handful of pigs and, in season, turkeys. Rod dispatches vegetable boxes to three-hundred local customers and up to four-thousand litres of soup each week to farm shops, cafés and delis.

Growing up in Kent as "a wayward child with too much energy", Rod often absconded to a nearby farm to help and to indulge his fascination with old farm machinery. He met Ben Mosely at agricultural college in the early nineties. "There was no talk of organic farming

– then they were banging on about sprays," he says. But he and Ben realised they shared a vision for working the land in step with nature. After initially going their separate ways: Ben to Indonesia with Voluntary Services Overseas to help set up a sustainable village food system, and Rod into metalwork and interior design, they reunited to take over Bickham Farm and then founded Rod and Ben's Soups.

Derelict when they arrived, the farm is now a flourishing sustainable system rich in wildlife, including rare Lesser Horseshoe bats, dormice and otters. Miles of typically dense Devon hedgerows accommodate an astounding array of species: ash, oak, spindle, blackthorn, elder, hawthorn and dog rose. Some pastures have never been ploughed and purple orchids, primroses and black knapweed thrive. Crops are rotated to maintain a healthy soil, as are animals to avoid parasite build-ups. The Dexters graze the Exminster Marshes, where tussocks they create attract breeding lapwings and their cowpats lure the scarce hornet robber fly. An ancient 'hollow way', a route carved by pilgrims and herders since Roman times, cuts through the farm, as does the more recent A38.

"One of the big myths is that using manufactured nitrogen fertiliser is helpful. It makes crops grow in

a different way, and you have to use lots of sprays to deal with the problems it creates," explains Rod testily. "But there is a natural cycle that can work very well without artificial input. It's a more positive approach."

Visitors and school groups can join farm walks, including one led by a herbalist to help identify medicinal plants, and visit the old cob threshing barn and resuscitated cider press. Rod also lays on an occasional communal feast in his 'rustic restaurant'. "The last one we did was fantastic. We toured the farm, ate too much and talked until one in the morning while the barn owls hooted; people loved it and it proves they don't want shiny restaurants and manufactured 'farm experiences.'"

In the Middle Ages English gardeners would have been familiar with around one-hundred-and-twenty different vegetables; by the 1970s they were cultivating fewer than fifty. Thanks to growers like Rod and Ben, the repertoire is on the rise again.

"Part of my job is putting new things in front of people," says Rod. "If they make the effort to cook strange things like kohlrabi or salsify, they will probably like them. Ultimately it's about taste – for example, beefsteak tomatoes are pretty ugly but have a beautiful flavour.

"Good vegetables make good soup," asserts Rod. "Ours are made with our own stock and herbs that we grow in summer and freeze." No artificial additives lurk inside his soups such as Leek & Potato, Red Pepper & Lime and, Rod's favourite, Chickpea & Spinach. Recipes come from Rod's mum and are cooked in small batches by chef David Jacobson.

After a successful eleven-year partnership, Ben left to take up a golden opportunity to run another organic farm; Rod continues the farm and the brand. "I leave the office work to others, though, and keep myself in the fields. It's safest!"

His deep respect for those who work the land includes a strong international perspective. Rod has visited fairtrade producers in Africa with his brother Matthew, better known as the comedian Harry Hill. He has spent time with organic

banana farmers in Ghana and peanut growers in Malawi. "You could see the benefit of the fairer price in a higher standard of living, so I always defend the higher prices of organic and fairtrade food. "The real cost of the cheap alternative is much higher, you just don't pay for it in the same way."

Heasley House

Heasley Mill South Molton
Devon EX36 3LE
01598 740213 www.heasley-house.co.uk

In a fold of the Mole Valley on the south-east edge of Exmoor, sits Heasley House, a Georgian mine captain's house. The setting and the country-house chic you might expect but the urbane menu is surprisingly sophisticated. There's an intriguing wine list, too, most of which are available by the glass, and there's a signature list of classic Burgundies and Bordeaux at astonishingly low prices.

Paul and Jan Gambrill had no experience of running a hotel when they took over Heasley House in 2004. "We spent twenty-five years in London teaching and in IT and then got to that age – fifty – where we questioned whether we wanted to carry on with our careers or move to the country for the rest of our lives," says Paul. Then, he was a passionate amateur cook and a seasoned hotel-and-restaurant guest in the course of his work for IBM.

He had clear ideas about what makes a memorable hotel. "I remember a place we stayed in Ireland: the food and wine were great, the atmosphere and service fantastic, and the bed comfy so it didn't matter that the bathroom and bedroom were a bit out-dated."

It took three years to find a house with Heasley's credentials: small enough (eight rooms) to run themselves with help, quiet but not remote, functional but in need of refurbishment. Since 2004 they have injected a lightness of touch without losing the Georgian proportions and grandness. They have created an atmospheric panelled bar with leather sofas and bold modern art on the walls and a dining room with space for twenty-four with a wood-burning stove.

"We didn't want to achieve 'fine dining' status but did want to exceed diners' expectations," says Paul. "It's a very personal service and no hands are held behind our backs as we pour the wine. We're usually on first-name terms with guests and there's banter between tables. Paul, our chef, usually delivers the cheese course which gives him a chance to meet his regulars. Provenance of food is what guests ask about, rather than whether it's produced sustainably or organic."

Says Paul: "I visit all our local suppliers. Meat and game comes from Exmoor; eggs from Hilary, just down the road; veal from a farmer on the Cornish border. Live lobsters come in from Tommy Perlham at Clovelly; they have such a reputation that guests ring ahead to check when they'll be on the menu. Fish, caught off Devon and Cornwall coasts, are on the menu the day after landing. Our salmon comes from a very good farm in Scotland."

Getting consistency in the quality of fruit and vegetables is a battle, although local potatoes, asparagus, root vegetables and brassica are generally good. "We work with whatever is in season but, inevitably, we'll have to pull in tomatoes from Holland." A newly installed polytunnel will provide salad crops and micro-greens, so they hope to have more home-grown produce. A healthy bartering system with locals ensures good supplies of Bramley apples, runner beans, blackberries and chutneys.

The wines, mostly from small vineyards that would never sell in high street multiples, include some from local vineyards such as the hugely-popular Camel Valley in Cornwall. "We price our wines very competitively to allow guests to not just play safe."

Menus are short and simple, full of classic dishes infused with flavours that you wouldn't get at home. So, it might be venison on parsnip purée with blueberry sauce or best end of Devon lamb with cannellini bean purée and thyme sauce. Fish is allowed to shine rather than be messed about with; puddings are classics; and you won't find foams or artistic smudges.

Paul happily admits to nicking ideas. "We do shut the hotel to eat out." They collect ideas on notebooks and iphone cameras to keep the surprises coming.

They run a tight but relaxed ship with Paul in the kitchen, Jan front-of-house and five part-time staff looking after the house and gardens. Waste avoidance is second nature to his staff; the hotel has six recycling bins and Paul is particularly anxious to avoid food waste. A glut of lobster might mean a costume change to lobster thermidor, luxury fish pie or lobster salad.

The quality of food is important but it's the whole package that determines whether a place works or not, believes Paul. "We don't go for perfection – that's boring. Relaxation is what we're into, and experimentation. We have a lot of fun."

Heasley House

Dinner, 2/3 courses £22/£28
Wines £10–£30
Closed February
Nearest train: Tiverton Parkway

The Cadeleigh Arms

Cadeleigh Tiverton
Devon EX16 8HP 01884 855238
www.thecadeleigharms.co.uk

The Cadeleigh Arms is a two-woman tour de force: Jane Dreyer is front-of-house, bar manager, maitre d', waitress and executive chef; business partner Elspeth Burrage, who commutes between here and her weekday job in London, is proprietor, strategist and marketing manager. Working alongside a small talented team in the kitchen and with weekend part-timers, it's a tightly run ship.

"As I am here on the floor every shift," says Jane, "it is my mission to create a business that enhances both the local area and its produce and at the same time encourages and develops our young team."

When the pair took over the rundown pub in 2006 they wanted to create a place "that showcased local produce, had style, was affordable and had a nice atmosphere. The sort of place we always searched for."

The feel now is stylishly rustic: low beamed ceilings, flagstone floors, raspberry red walls, log fires, polished wooden mismatched tables, books, chessboard, children's games. And the clientele's eclectic: people that live and work here rub shoulders with townies and academics, lunching ladies, shooting parties or university students and their visiting families.

"We're not trying to be a poncey restaurant," explains Jane. "We offer traditional food with a contemporary twist, at a reasonable cost." They want the place to be a community pub with a strong sense of ownership and involvement. The strikingly colourful art on the walls, for example, is by a local artist; their staff are local (frequently, sons and daughters of suppliers); they use

a local husband-and-wife marketing business; and the pub's skittle alley is used for charity events, wine tastings and theatre performances.

Meat, game, venison and poultry come from within five miles; sausages from Simply Sausage, seasonal fruit and vegetables from local farm shops, daily (non-frozen) fish deliveries from St Ives; herbs from the pub's garden. They use the most local businesses they can for things such as ice creams and preserves.

Neither will they always go for organic, regardless. "Sometimes there will be an additional cost and we have to think about how much extra customers would be prepared to pay," explains Jane.

Being governed by seasonality goes some way to

keeping costs down. In the autumn, for example, the cinnamon pannacotta will be served with roasted local plums; an abundance of partridge might inspire a warm salad with chestnuts and pears; Jane will forage for blackberries or sloes to make a fragrant gin.

The Cadeleigh Arms is in one of England's prime counties for home-produced alcohol: cider, scrumpy and fruit juices come from the apples of Sandford Orchards at Crediton; wine from Yearlstone at Bickleigh, Devon's oldest vineyard; hand-pulled real ales from Otter Brewery near Honiton.

There are daily changes to the menu but there'd be an outcry if their Bangers & Mash (all ingredients coming from within a three-mile radius) or their golden homemade pie were removed.

"Everybody says they feel at home here," says Jane. "They don't just come for a meal and a drink. They come for a chat." There is a genuine collective desire to help each others' businesses prosper.

Jane worked with owner Barny Butterfield of Sandford Orchards to develop a homemade ginger beer

and she recommends the afternoon tea and wine tours at Yearlstone Vineyard; they, in turn, send visitors to the pub. "And we pass on recipes to customers to inspire people to use local produce in a different way." Jane and Elspeth are particularly pleased that many of their suppliers are regulars at the pub.

"Our customers are our friends, and we want them to feel comfortable, well cared for and looked after. But," Jane adds, "it's a two-way thing. We can provide the food and the setting but we only remain here if people come in." Sustaining a good country pub requires commitment on both sides.

The Cadeleigh Arms

Evening main courses £9.95–£17.95
Dining club membership available
No food on Sunday evening or on Monday
Nearest train: Tiverton Parkway

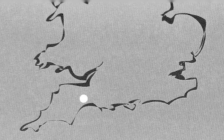

Combe House Devon

Gittisham Honiton
Exeter EX14 3AD 01404 540 400
www.combehousedevon.com

Combe House brims with the heart and soul that owners Ken and Ruth Hunt pour into it. They are proud of their renovation of this grand Elizabethan manor near Honiton in Devon but, most of all, they cherish the relationships they've built, with staff, guests, suppliers and the wider community.

"We used to work in large corporate hotels, where pressure to make profit for shareholders reduced all relationships to mean minimums," says Ken. "Here, we've discovered a wonderful new world of generous relationships and real hospitality. We're most proud of our extended family of thirty-eight staff, which intertwines the life of the hotel with that of the village."

Breakfast, available to non-residents too, exemplifies the Hunts' and chef Hadleigh Barrett's philosophy. Juices, if not their own apple, pear or rhubarb, are from a local organic producer. Teas and coffees are fairtrade. Everything from croissants to marmalade is made in-house, with smoked haddock and kippers from a traditional Devon smokehouse, and butter from an artisan dairy. Eggs are free-range, tomatoes from the greenhouse, amber honey from the hives.

Homely it may be, but dinner is elegant: amuse-bouches – dainty spoons of quail rillettes with home-pickled cornichons, shots of warm foie gras custard with chestnut foam, individual basil ravioli in tomato water moats – might precede celeriac panna cotta with marinated raisins and roasted cobnuts, seared bass with confit peppers and sauce vièrge, and poached pear with pear sorbet and pistachio ice cream.

Groups can book the painstakingly restored Georgian kitchen dining room, with a functioning log-burning cast iron range, string of copper pans and candles and oil lamps in place of electricity; this room also hosts staff lunch – as it would have done in the eighteenth century – a time when conversations about work and life overlap.

"At first we were naïve," admits Ken. "We thought 'local' meant using the local greengrocer and butcher, wherever the food came from. We've since dug deeper to find producers whose principles we endorse, and whose products are honest and evocative of local traditions. We want to help bring back the cultural heritage of food."

Lasting just six weeks, Combe House's spring lamb season creates a stir. Organic Dorset Down lambs from Blacklake Farm provide Sunday leg roasts, slow-cooked shoulders, rosemary-stuffed saddles, seared loins and rillettes. "This is true spring lamb, a flavour I remember from long ago. The Broomfields don't force lambing in December to make the Easter market. Their lambs come later, so they feed on spring grasses and taste incredible."

Unendangered fish, such as pollack, bream, brill, gurnard and line-caught bass reach the kitchen within hours of being unloaded from day-boats at Looe and Brixham. In summer live pot-caught lobsters and crabs arrive twice a week from a friend in the Scilly Isles.

"Over-fishing terrifies me, like over-foresting and over-farming," says Ken. "We're destroying our seas and soils and putting nothing back except man-made rubbish. We must help avoid catastrophe."

Ten acres of lawns, ancient cedars, paddocks, orchards and woodland are maintained with minimal use of pesticides and no artificial fertilisers. Compost, leaf mould and horse muck feed four walled Victorian kitchen gardens. There are flageolet and borlotti beans; globe and Jerusalem artichokes; cabbages for all seasons; year-round supplies of shallots and garlic; currants, strawberries and Worcesterberries; dozens of herbs.

Summer's end heralds a flurry of preserving. The two-hundred-and-fifty-year-old mulberry tree gives fruit for jam, the quince's heavy fruits are boiled into ruby-red membrillo to pair with West Country cheeses, gherkins are pickled, gooseberry cordial bottled, cobnuts stored

and grapes from the century-old vine pressed for juice. They even cure pancetta and prosciutto-style hams.

Ken and Ruth are committed to sustainable hospitality and use a raft of measures to lower water and energy use, reduce waste, recycle, limit food miles, use natural building materials and encourage wildlife, including rare lesser and greater horseshoe bats.

"Most of all, what we do here is create long-lasting, meaningful relationships," says Ken. "A lot of those relationships centre on food and the healthiest, most pleasurable and least destructive ways of enjoying it. Our future might depend on it."

Combe House Devon

Dinner, 3 courses with canapés, £48
Mon-Sat lunch, 2/3 courses with canapés, £25/£29
Food always available
Nearest train: Honiton

BridgeHouse Hotel

3 Prout Bridge Beaminster
Dorset DT8 3AY
01308 862200 www.bridge-house.co.uk

The Donovans' move to Beaminster had the makings of a docu-soap: two high-fliers ditch their cosmopolitan lifestyle to live the rural dream and take on a hotel. They had to work together and learn about running a restaurant and hotel, all while having their first baby. Mark, previously a television director, had producer friends queuing up to shoot it. "I had the good sense to say no. We had no idea what we were doing!"

BridgeHouse's reputation rests on its food. The abundant West Country larder amply supplies the brasserie-style restaurant so there is a strong Dorset twist to the often gallic cooking. Chefs delight in the Ruby Red beef, hand-dived Lyme Bay scallops, Denhay farmhouse cheddar and local cider.

The Donovans discovered BridgeHouse while renovating their holiday home in Netherbury. "We'd fantasise about running a place, never thinking we would. One evening while we were eating there the manager let slip that the hotel was coming up for sale. Jo and I looked at each other and both instantly saw our chance."

The Donovans got more than they bargained for when they took over the thirteenth-century hamstone house six years ago. "We hadn't appreciated how all-consuming the restaurant and the renovations would be." Their first move was to banish the outdated peach-coloured tablecloths and curtains; the ancient plumbing and awkward kitchen were next.

Now BridgeHouse is known for the way uncompromising quality – from the luxury soaps to chocolate truffles – melds with cosy informality and a lack of pretension. Manager Jane Fox and her husband Colin have worked here for twenty years and make a redoubtable double-act: Jane knows many of her customers and will rearrange whole seating plans to accommodate their quirks; Colin pours drinks in the homely bar and puts all at ease.

The warmth and atmosphere of the twin oak-beamed parlours, each with gigantic inglenook fireplace, encourage you to linger but the real rewards await at your table – in either the candle-lit Georgian wood-panelled dining room, in a conservatory overlooking the walled

garden, or on the covered terrace. Talented chef Linda Paget brought the Donovans invaluable local culinary know-how. The delicious Dorset apple cake is made the way her grandmother taught her thirty years ago, her lamb baked in hay and Netherbury cider is a popular Sunday special.

Executive chef Steve Pielesz increasingly holds the reins and brings flavours from his Michelin-starred restaurant days in France. He prepares Fowey River moules marinière, Cornish bouillabaisse, West Bay lobster and, occasionally, mackerel caught on his father's boat. "Most seafood is caught at night and on plates by lunch-time," Mark says.

West Country meat comes from butcher Chris Rawles in Bridport, who also rears his own free-range pork. Denhay Farm provides a delectable prosciutto-like ham, cured in Bramley apple juice, salts and herbs, then smoked over beech wood and air-dried on the bone for a year. Free-range eggs have come from Sally Vickery in Beaminster for over a decade. Lavender to infuse the crème brûlée is from the garden. Colin, a keen mushroom

forager, occasionally presents the kitchen with the challenge of enormous puffballs.

The cheese course is impressive: Cornish Yarg wrapped in nettles, Somerset Brie, Denhay cheddar and Dorset Blue Vinney; the name of the blue cheese comes from 'vinew', meaning mould, and once it was made in almost every Dorset farmhouse.

Mark cannot resist the ham hock and foie gras terrine with homemade chutney, followed by pan-fried calf's liver with bacon, mash and homemade jus. "Heaven on a plate!" For Jo, the mushrooms on tagliatelle with truffle oil are irresistible. Breads, biscuits, ice creams and sorbets are made from scratch; the strawberry and black pepper ice cream is superb.

West Dorset is a culinary destination, with Hugh Fearnley-Whittingstall's River Cottage near Axminster, Mark Hix's Oyster and Fish House in Lyme Regis, and Masterchef winner Mat Follas's restaurant, the Wild Garlic, on Beaminster square. Food-lovers head to nearby Bridport for its bustling monthly farmers' market or a tour of Palmers Brewery that has made ale since 1794. Local cooking classes range from 'stress-free entertaining' with Lesley Waters to 'pig in a day' at River Cottage. Mark can organise mushroom hunting and fishing excursions, too.

Mark and Jo's son Louis, now six, has had an impact: children's meals are as carefully prepared as the restaurant meals, organic ingredients are most often used and fresh fruit and vegetable purees are made for babies to make life relaxing for those staying over with children.

"In the house's seven-hundred-year timeline we're just a dot, but I hope a significant one." Despite the hard work, the Donovans haven't looked back and both are still enchanted by the bountiful Hardy Country. "It's luscious. There's so much here for the taking."

BridgeHouse Hotel

Evening main courses £10–£21.50
Two-course brasserie lunch £18
Food available seven days a week
Nearest train: Crewkerne

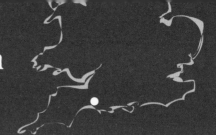

Becklands Organic Farm

Whitchurch Canonicorum Bridport
Dorset DT6 6RG 01297 560298
www.becklandsorganicfarm.co.uk

Becklands Farm is in the rolling hills of Dorset's Jurassic Coast, in stunningly beautiful countryside laced with old hedgerows. The Blue Lias soil, heavy with clay, is far better suited to livestock than crops. Most farms in the area are small family affairs passed down through generations, which Hilary Joyce speculates is due to the fact that the area's feudal system never existed here, as William the Conqueror gifted the territory to his chaplain and it remained in the Church's hands until the Reformation.

The Joyces – she a public relations consultant from London and Francis a Dorset farmer – took over Francis' father's thirty-acre farm near Lyme Regis in 1995; Francis harnesses his decades of experience to manage the land and animals and Hilary is the marketeer.

Long ago Hilary was part of a team selling 'plastic' cheese for a large American brand; now she enthuses about pheasants and rabbits scurrying from hedgerows, buzzards soaring above, clouds of butterflies springing from fields of wild flowers, and the superb flavour of grass-fed pedigree beef.

Hilary believes the farm's forty-five-plus organic years account for its astounding biodiversity and health. "Our soil teems with worms, the badger sett has been here

for centuries, we've never had a TB reactor and our vet's bill is virtually nothing. We have rare cirl buntings here, too, a small bird that many thought disappeared from Dorset for thirty-five years."

The White Leghorn hens and Devon Ruby Reds follow each other around the pastures, as their wild ancestors would have done millennia ago. The cows trim the grass to a height appreciated by the foraging chickens, whose potent natural fertiliser boosts the greenery for the cattle the following year.

"The rotation keeps the land and animals healthy and our beef and eggs are of such high quality because the animals live so naturally. We haven't had to raise prices in two years because our cows are not grain fed; cows eating grain or processed cake to me seems very odd."

The Joyces work closely with the local abattoir and sell their beef themselves; Hilary predicts that in time people will expect to see meat on menus with details of age, breed and provenance, as we do for wine.

"Few so-called 'free-range' chickens run around on grass," explains Hilary, "they are often with thousands of others in a barn, too densely packed to realise there's a pop hole to the outside. With Soil Association eggs you are guaranteed that the hens are free-range."

Francis pioneered free-range eggs in the sixties and seventies, when foods like Angel Delight and Smash were considered socially superior and safer. At first he had to take his eggs to health food shops in Exeter. Now sales are booming at the farm gate and through a local box scheme, and B&B guests enjoy them each morning.

Unlike their battery cousins, Becklands hens are allowed a month of lie-ins in midwinter, when artificial light is not used to keep them feeding and laying. "Eggs used to be scarcer and more expensive in winter," remembers Hilary, "We've got so spoiled, having everything all the time." Prolific egg eating was not common in Britain until the introduction of large poultry farms. Francis will tell you it takes a hen as much energy to lay an egg a day as it does a woman to deliver twins twice a week. "Caged hens lay into a conveyor belt so their eggs are immediately whisked away, but hens like to stand up and have a look. Francis thinks they go neurotic if they can't see the product of their labour."

Raised in London, Hilary understood how little city folk know of their food's provenance, so she set up guided walks for visitors, much to the amusement of her husband and neighbouring farmers who thought everyone knew it all already. The walks are hugely popular.

Visitors marvel at the natural beauty, but Hilary reminds visitors that most food originates in factory farms, where cows have callused feet from concrete floors and skiploads of exhausted hens are jettisoned weekly. "Some have this idea of the idyllic countryside, like a Hovis ad, but farming is full of tensions and many farmers are unwell." Francis suffers from a rare cancer caused by a weedkiller he used as a young farmhand so Hilary is shocked by farmers who resist EU attempts to ban dangerous agrichemicals.

The Joyces make fertiliser from comfrey – also known as 'knitbone' – used medicinally for centuries. Its deep roots mine nutrients which can be harvested from its decomposed leaves. "It smells like sewage," says Hilary, "so when we sell it to others we only send cuttings in the post. We wouldn't be popular if a bottle broke."

The garden harbours other quintessentially English plants – medlar, quince, marrow, blackberry, crab apple and elderflower – with which Hilary concocts traditional jams, jellies and cordials. Her creative side, once channelled into corporate business, is nurtured by the possibilities for creating things inspired by her surroundings. The farm shop also sells her pressed flower cards, ceramics and a novel about a twelfth-century West Dorset abbot. Hilary loves music and she plays 'The Five Seasons' by Cecilia McDowall for visitors, a choral piece inspired by organic farms, including Becklands.

Gaggle of Geese
Buckland Newton Dorchester
Dorset DT2 7BS
01300 345249 www.thegaggle.co.uk

"A good pub serves good food, good drink and good fun and belongs to the community. We are only custodians." Here in the village of Buckland Newton, the Gaggle of Geese does just that. As well as welcoming visitors to the area, it's watering hole, restaurant, meeting place and market place for all locals, from the Lord and his tractor driver to poultry breeders, pensioners, skittlers and morris dancers.

Mark, chef proprietor, and wife Emily grew up surrounded by food and farming, and worked in several pubs, before returning home to Dorset to distil everything they'd learnt and loved into transforming, first, the European Inn in Piddletrenthide and then the Gaggle of Geese. "When they experienced the new lease of life enjoyed by the European, locals persuaded us to buy the Gaggle and resurrect it."

Within months the staff increased from one to thirty-five, homely sofas congregated around the fireplace, wood panelling (complete with drinkers' propping ledge) flanked the extensive bar, and a menagerie of sheep, hens, geese and goats took up residence in the paddock.

"First-timers sometimes leave after five seconds, thinking they've accidentally walked into someone's home; others sit for hours with coffee and newspapers, or just pop in for Dorset rarebit to tide them over until dinner. Em's always here, holding court," smiles Mark.

The menu reflects Mark's love of classic comfort food – honey-roast ham with eggs and chips, pork sausages with bubble and squeak, slow-roasted pork shoulder with pan haggerty and apple sauce, homemade burgers and chicken Kiev. Mediterranean starters "add some sunshine": roasted red pepper hummus, peaches wrapped in ham,

courgette soup with basil pesto, bruschetta topped with liver, chorizo and capers.

"My mother and grandmother taught me to cook from scratch, so everything here is, except ketchup and HP sauce. My squirrelling instinct has us making kilos of preserves from our orchard fruit and villagers' gluts – spiced pear chutney, green tomato chutney, strawberry jam – which we sell too. I buy whole animals as it helps the farmer and gives me lots to play with," enthuses Mark who, unlike many, relishes the lengthy process of making Bath chaps from pigs' cheeks.

Hogget and mutton come from Mark's father's farm ten miles away, and organic pork from nearby Sydling Brook farm. Beef from local butcher Simon Harvell is properly hung and usually from heifers. "They put on fat intramuscularly, so they are tastier, whereas the boys grow pot bellies ," explains Mark. Game is supplied by a trio of farmers who try to keep up with the demand for pan-fried pigeon breast with red wine jus.

Vegetables arrive from an organic smallholding, and villagers' gardens. "It's not unusual to find boxes of courgettes and beans left on the step, or buckets of mackerel from fishermen. Once we found forty pheasants hanging in the shed," says Mark. In their mission to keep pounds in the local economy, the Hammicks buy olives cured in Sturminster Newton, stock Sherborne Castle wines and serve Blue Vinny, smoked Dorset Red and Woolsery goat's cheeses with Dorset biscuits and Piddle Valley honey.

The pub's name derives from its twice annual poultry fair, at which livestock is auctioned, raising several thousand pounds for charity. "We make a real party of it, with farmers' market, hog roast, cider tent and cream teas," says Mark. Emily wants to expand the farmers' market, too.

On the twenty-ninth of September, when peasants used to keep landlords sweet and, therefore, their rents down with the gift of a goose, the Hammicks hold a Michaelmas feast. Their pet geese are spared, while birds from Michael Coleman in Milton Abbas take centre stage: warm goose liver and giblet salad, followed by goose leg confit with pan-fried breast and potatoes.

Barely a month passes without some event or other

taking place here – maybe the parish pensioners' lunch, the primary school's Christmas dinner, village fête, autumn barbecues and a Christmas fair. "Just trying to make money is boring," reflects Mark. "We're part of the community so want what we do to contribute. This is our social life, too, and we want to have fun."

Gaggle of Geese

Evening main courses £8–£15
Lunchtime sandwiches and ploughman's available
No food on Christmas Day
Nearest trains: Sherborne and Dorchester

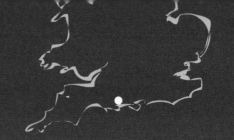

Dorset Oysters
Poole Dorset BH17 0GB
01202 666057
www.dorsetoysters.com

Pete Miles left school to work on the pilot boats that guide ships in and out of Poole Harbour. "I was around fishermen and enjoyed fishing. I then started to catch prawns with my homemade pots and supplied them to London restaurants and meeting the chefs inspired me to open my own seafood restaurant, Storm, in Poole." His intention was to specialise in oysters but, although the harbour yields four-hundred tonnes of oysters each year, he had to serve Irish oysters.

Then, Othniel Oysters in Poole was the first and only certified organic shellfish farm in the UK and owner Gary Wordsworth was exporting to France, China and elsewhere in Britain. "Part of the problem was it was difficult to get Othniel's oysters locally." So in 2008 Pete built his own high-tech purification plant, bought Gary's oysters, cleansed them in his plant using UV light and started selling them locally.

Making ethical choices when buying seafood is complicated, as it depends on season, provenance and catching or farming practice as well as species. The Marine Conservation Society (MCS) helpfully rates seafood from one (most sustainable) to five (to avoid).

"The fish business is a scary thing – lots of take and not much putting back," says Pete. "The old boys in the harbour have seen the decline in their lifetimes." He'll also tell you how eleven pounds of baby fish are caught to produce one pound of farmed salmon and how pigs and chickens are the biggest fish eaters (via dry feed).

Farmed oysters score one, as the baby oysters, called spats, come from hatcheries not the wild. Othniel's organically certified oysters feed purely on natural algae and no additives or chemicals are used at any stage. Gary's specially designed 'eco-harvester' boat is gentle on both seabed and oysters. "It's like working with soil," explains Pete, "we need to protect the fragile substrate." Oyster farms can actually improve the ecosystem by acting as a giant filter; Gary's stock filters the equivalent of two-hundred-and-fifty Olympic swimming pools a day.

The farming of oysters dates back to at least Roman or Greek times. For millennia people have believed in their health-giving properties: Parisians and Londoners used to buy oysters by the hundred, Cicero ate them to nourish his eloquence and Louis XI swallowed them by prescription. Oysters are now known to be rich in minerals, vitamins and cancer-fighting ceramides.

Oyster farming has slowly increased in Britain, but we have never fully regained our love of the slippery bivalve; we export the majority, along with most native shellfish, and frozen prawns from Asia seem to have grabbed most of the market. Trawled wild tiger prawns have a MCS score of five, not least because up to ten kilograms of by-catch is discarded for every kilogram of prawns landed.

Pete is exasperated by this madness. "Supermarket fish counters are generally poor, stocking fish flown in from around the world. In the Poole area they prefer to offer Scottish or Irish oysters when they have some of the best oysters in the country caught here. Their prices are high, too, so it's not surprising we eat so much less fish than the French and Spanish." Pete's purification plant has capacity for fifty-thousand oysters a week and selling up to six-thousand a week.

"An oyster's appearance, texture and flavour depends on where it grew," explains Pete. "We have an unusual double tide here, meaning the water is exceptionally clean and rich in food, so our oysters grow fast. They sit on the seabed, open up and scoff all day. They are full and plump, with a good balance of salt and mineral flavour." Pete loves to coat his oysters in a light tempura batter, deep fry and then swoop them through a soy and ginger dip. "I like them raw, too, with just a dash of lemon. An oyster should flinch when the juice hits it, which shows it's alive."

"Here we have an unusual double tide, meaning the water is exceptionally clean and rich in food, so our oysters grow fast"

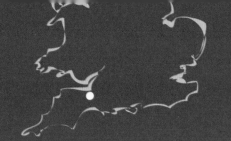

John Ridout's father came to Huntstile in 1950 as a tenant farmer. In 1979 John inherited the tenancy and took on the seven-hundred acres of rolling fields in the Quantock foothills. He bought the then ramshackle farmers' lodgings from the landlord and soon discovered how expensive it is to restore and maintain a beautiful six-hundred-year-old farmhouse. To help pay the bills John and partner Lizzie Myers opened log cabins, cottages and a campsite for guests and bed and breakfast rooms within the house.

John's brother-in-law, soil expert Richard Plowright, began growing organic vegetables at Huntstile for his box scheme and was John's inspiration to convert the substantial part of their holding over to the organic production of wheat, barley and oats for well-known cereal brands. Prosaically one of their biggest challenges is keeping on top of the weeds.

"The seed bank of, say, dock weed in the soil takes forty years to run dry; our other challenge is our organic wild oats have to be hand-rogued and that is labour-intensive. Eight of us spent June doing that." No wonder

then that organic breakfast cereals cost more.

Six-foot-tall organic milk thistles are grown for their seeds, which are ground and used in natural liver cleansing remedies. "We're the only organic milk thistle producers in England, and we know why now," says John. "They spread like wildfire and have their own personal armour of steel spikes. You can't get near them." So much

for the innocent image of the daisy family. Horse chestnuts, borage and marigolds are grown for alternative remedies, too. "The deep red loamy sand is so fertile it will grow anything." says John.

The British Whites, pedigree cattle claiming ancient origins, stand out with their comical black noses, ears and socks. They grow slowly and make excellent beef, perfect for Lizzie's Sunday roasts.

Lizzie has created a small restaurant that is open Thursday to Saturday and Sunday lunch by reservation and runs sausage-, cake- and bread-making courses, too.

Cooking has always been a passion. "I made cakes with my grandmother and helped my grandfather who was a keen vegetable gardener. The Greek family next door grew aubergines, artichokes and peppers in polytunnels and cooked up garden snails." So Lizzie was exposed young to flavours rarely found in late-sixties Britain.

Lizzie keeps chickens and, unlike the cattle destined for the table, each of her birds is individually named. "They can identify up to sixty other chickens themselves, by the shape of their heads and way they move, so that's the maximum number I keep," explains Lizzie, who also

gives lots of chicken-health advice to other owners. There are three huge pet sows and two rescued goats, too. Children like to feed and stroke the animals, and collect the eggs. "Much of our food waste goes to our pigs and chickens. Our eggs are fantastic!"

Lizzie spends much of her day cooking. After her "Gordon moment", as assistants call the frantic half hour preceding dinner, wonderful spreads of robustly flavoured food appear, often garnished with violets, marigolds, pansies and borage from the kitchen garden. The beef, eggs, fruit and vegetables will most likely be from the farm. "Making organic produce available to the community in which it is grown is key. Supermarkets have removed that opportunity for so many farmers."

Lizzie promotes her philosophy by cooking up an annual feast for the community specifically to showcase all the excellent food grown in the area. Perhaps the best campaigns are the delicious ones?

"The whole ecology of food needs to be revalued," she says. "We shouldn't fly food all round the world every day. Kenyans should be growing crops for their families and villages, not producing fine beans for Tesco in Basildon."

The Magdalen Project

Magdalen Farm Winsham Chard
Somerset TA20 4PA 01460 30144
www.themagdalenproject.org.uk

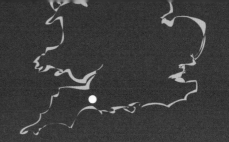

Sausages, bread, cheese, cider and chutney – just a few of the things you can learn how to make at the Magdalen Project. First-time smallholders, whose dreams of The Good Life are hitting reality, come here for guidance on everything from lambing to hedge-laying and skills once commonplace – keeping hens, weaving willow, meat-curing, preserving – are taught by Magdalen's experts.

"We live in a society which is unsustainable in many ways, so we're doing our bit to change that. Self-sufficiency skills are going to become increasingly important," says director Giles Aspinall.

The project – also known as the Wessex Foundation – was the brainchild of a serial social entrepreneur and sustainability guru. He bought Magdalen Farm and converted the derelict nineteenth-century milking sheds into an education centre, that now hosts nearly seven-thousand visitors a year. The charity offers a range of activities and courses which promote sustainability, respect for the environment and healthy lifestyles.

The organic farm's one hundred and thirty-two acres spill over from Dorset into Somerset, and almost reach Devon to the west; views are stunning in all directions. Beef cattle, sheep, pigs, goats and chickens multiply as fast as finances allow. "It would be unethical not to use the land to produce food, so we're expanding vegetable plots to supply our kitchen, and will sell surpluses through two community-run village shops.

"Britain is full of gardens and the potential for growing more food here is huge," says Giles. "Elsewhere in Europe keeping a goat and chickens in the yard is still common – they're low maintenance, eat scraps and

"Probably because everyone told me not to!" laughs Phil. "The business would be more profitable in a wealthier area but we wanted to stick our necks out and be here. Sixty-five per cent of customers come by foot or bike, so we reach local families."

Phil and others with a shared vision have launched his biggest initiative to-date: a fifty-acre community farm twelve miles south of Bristol, overlooking the serene Chew Valley Lake. The idea behind it is not only to significantly increase the proportion of local produce in the veg boxes and the shop, but to involve as many as possible in growing it.

The group has worked with landowner Luke Hasell to develop a not-for-profit company. Members pay a fee, commit to at least one day a year helping on the farm, and get discounted produce.

"It's brilliant!" enthuses Phil. "We'll hope to be collecting groups in a bus – corporate employees, families, schoolchildren, people with learning disabilities, community groups – and put them together on the farm." Volunteers will dig, plant, weed and harvest "everything it's possible to grow here"; some will corral the kids and others will prepare lunch. "Using volunteers on the land is not about saving money but about creating the heart and soul of the farm."

Phil is determined to reduce the community farm's carbon footprint and volunteers will take the place of some of the farm machinery. "Using huge machines may be financially efficient, but reliance on petroleum in farming is unsustainable."

Phil rants against what he terms "industrial organic" that he feels can reduce food's heart and soul and hopes the community farm will provide a toolkit for the future. "We need to make radical choices now. There is no time left, you can feel the effects of global warming every day."

Eating purely seasonal British produce is one such radical option. "There'd be enough food, we'd just need to adjust our diets and tastes, and return to home preserving." But how to tempt people away from the booming fast food culture, which uses highly processed ingredients from all over the globe? Phil believes exposing children to nature is key and he works with many schools.

"Seeing food growing and touching and tasting it – that's what sparks a child's interest," he says. "There's a magic to eating food fresh from the land. I can't describe it, but my God I can feel it."

The Marlborough Tavern

35 Marlborough Buildings Bath
Bath & NE Somerset BA1 2LY 01225 423731
www.marlborough-tavern.com

Standing in a muddy field, their pub just in view behind, proprietors Joe Cussens and Justin Sleath and their entire staff – from kitchen porter to barman – taste raw turnips and swedes being yanked from the ground. This is the annual staff visit to seventh generation market gardener, Mike Eades, who harvests vegetables before dawn so they can be cooked at the Marlborough Tavern that day.

"We work closely with a great bunch of local suppliers who share our passion for exceptional food. They want to know their produce will be treated with respect and turned into inspiring dishes. And their enthusiasm and encyclopaedic knowledge rub off on our staff, who then appreciate all their hard work. There are fewer grumbles

Many of the salvaged tables and chairs come from Wood Works, a charity that trains unemployed people in furniture restoration. "We wanted to recreate that feeling of dining at a friend's house. Everyone feels welcome here, from students to pensioners," says Joe, who has always enjoyed throwing together dinner parties.

Food is essentially British and seasonal – for example broad bean, bacon, radish and mint salad in summer, wild mallard with cherry sauce, pickled walnuts and kale in winter. Chef Richard Knighting, who trained under Marco Pierre White in London, maintains a core menu of regulars' favourites – properly aged steaks with hand-cut chips, homemade beef burgers, slow-roast pork belly, chocolate bread and butter pudding. Daily specials, such

if deliveries are a little late and our staff can inform customers with confidence."

Friends since school, Joe and Justin quit their careers in advertising and retail in 2006 to take over the down-and-out Georgian boozer tucked behind Bath's Royal Crescent. Now, olive green wood panelling, local artwork and large windows create a traditional yet stylish feel.

as stuffed courgette flowers with chickpea, walnut and sage fritters, or roast loin and liver of venison with Cumberland sauce, give variety.

"Richard is passionate about his network of producers, and relentless in his attention to detail," says Joe. "For example he'll offer four different roasts for Sunday lunch, and make a different, perfectly paired, gravy from scratch for each, using proper stocks. Customers might not realise he's taken that trouble, but they notice it tastes delicious."

Meat comes from a host of local farms, acknowledged on the menu, with much from Neston Park Estate near Atworth, where beef, pork and lamb is reared to organic standards. Their game, shot on the estate, is celebrated at occasional game nights: roast pheasant with Brussels sprouts, chestnuts and whisky cream sauce; black pudding stuffed ballotine of rabbit with truffled leeks; confit breast of partridge with celeriac, bacon and mustard cress salad.

Seafood favours sustainable options: beer-battered hake, whiting or pollack with piquant caper mayonnaise;

need to be shipped or flown thousands of miles to reach us. We ask our fish merchants what's fresh in the market and create dishes around what they recommend, rather than devising dishes and hunting down the fish no matter what," explains Joe.

Back at the market garden, staff thank several generations of Eades for their dedication and move on to nearby Marshfield Farm to see the farm's own milk being made into the clotted cream and raspberry pavlova ice creams they serve at the Tavern. Tastings continue at the Fine Cheese Company, back in the centre of the city and the day finishes with a talk – and tasting – on food and wine pairing. Staff retention is not a problem at the Marlborough Tavern.

cuttlefish braised in its own ink; handlined black bream with spicy chorizo and salsa verde; fat chunks of diver-speared plaice.

"Our customers expect sustainable fish, and so do we. But it's not black and white. Some fish farming heavily pollutes the local ecosystem, but in other cases it's the better option. And some sustainable wild stocks would

The Marlborough Tavern

Evening main courses £10.95–£15.95
Regular food events and wine tastings
Food always available
Nearest train: Bath Spa

Pig's cheeks and trotters; lamb's livers and sweetbreads; ox hearts, shins and tails. All were once cooked in British homes and are now served in the most fashionable restaurants and gastropubs. "By using everything from snout to tail we keep prices down," explains Charlie Digney, co-owner of this small Georgian freehouse in Bath. "We avoid food waste and help farmers who need to sell whole animals. And it's all delicious."

Charlie and Amanda have since bought two more pubs: the Garrick's Head by the Theatre Royal in Bath and the Oakhill Inn near Shepton Mallet in Somerset. Linking all three is a passion for food. "High quality ingredients come before profit. We use the same suppliers as

here and in doing so we are lowering food miles," says Charlie. "We want to bridge gaps between producers and consumers, which is the essence of Slow food. If I bought Brazilian beef I wouldn't be able to chat to the farmer and check the quality."

In the laid-back bar, stylish with floor-length heavy brocade curtains and junk-shop gilded mirrors, a cosmopolitan crowd enjoy local ales and ciders; Cask-conditioned ale from the Digney's microbrewery at Oakhill hit the taps in 2010. Comforting dishes include cauliflower cheese soup, boiled bacon with cabbage, devilled lamb's kidneys, mutton chops with crispy potatoes, and creamed pearl barley with house-smoked garlic and Montgomery cheddar – a British 'risotto'.

Michelin-starred restaurants, and should probably charge more, but the fact that we use whole animals and share them between the pubs means we can keep prices down."

Most ingredients are sourced in and around Bath and all manner of fruits and vegetables come from Charlie's own allotment and friend Gerald Rich's market garden. "It would be a crime not to support the fantastic farmers

Upstairs, white tablecloths and silver candlesticks calm the mood. Walls carry images of Jane Grigson's regional guides to British cookery, published in 1984. "Grigson championed English food, and we're trying to do the same," says Charlie.

"England always had a fine cuisine, it's just been forgotten. For example, when food became industrialised

we turned to the Continent for quality products like salamis, but England has a long curing tradition."

Neil Creese, the head chef at the Oakhill Inn, makes sausages, ham, bacon and black pudding for all three pubs and head chef Adi Ware at the King William loves reinventing his grandparents' recipes: citrus and honey glazed ham hock with port-braised red cabbage, pot-roasted guinea fowl with lentils and bacon, braised beef shin and oxtail with mustard mash.

"Slow-cooking tougher cuts and using offal and game were common then," says Adi. "It baffles me that more people don't cook like that at home now, as it's much cheaper. All it takes is a little planning. Our salt beef goes in the oven at midnight and comes out in the morning

terrines, legs confited in fat, livers and hearts flash-fried to pile on toast, and carcasses brewed for broth. Lamb might be served three ways on one plate and rare beef steak which spent minutes over heat is paired with velvety shin stewed gently for hours. They make their own vinegar, jellies, chutneys and ice cream, and even smoke and pickle fish.

To keep prices down, seafood dishes favour mackerel, herring, sardines, hake, grey mullet, gurnard, trout and mussels. Charlie is mindful of avoiding unsustainable fish. "We have to persuade people to try these lesser known fish and steer them away from things like tuna, monkfish, turbot and cod. Most, once they have tried them, love them and come back for more."

beautifully tender – Sunday lunch sorted!"

Menus avoid foreign words, so panna cotta is 'set vanilla cream', gravadlax 'cured salmon' and cullen skink 'smoked haddock chowder'. Dishes may read and look simple, but benefit from considerable skill and time poured into them behind the scenes.

Ducks' breasts are smoked or transformed into

King William Pub and Dining Rooms

Evening main courses £12–£18
Two-/three-course weekday lunch £15/£20
No food Monday lunchtime
Nearest train: Bath Spa

63

The Mill at Gordleton

Silver Street Sway Lymington
Hampshire SO41 6DJ 01590 682219
www.themillatgordleton.co.uk

The Mill is a big operation. There are seven full-time chefs and over a hundred diners on busy days. And everything – "apart from the sausages because we're not very good at those" – is made here. Menus change weekly or seasonally but there's always the flexibility to take in unexpected produce.

Liz Cottingham, who owns and runs the four-hundred-year-old Mill near Lymington, also oversees the two acres of pretty gardens and thrives on the challenge. "In previous jobs I've never stayed more than two years. I'd take on the challenge, turn it around and then move

Now, they ask questions. They've found an organic vegetable supplier, their pork comes from a nearby farm, beef from Dorset and they're investigating a lamb supplier in the Isle of Wight. Goats' cheeses come from the village, organic flour from a local mill, and fish, crabs and lobsters from the Solent six miles away, plus the Mill has its own herb garden and greenhouse vegetables.

Her chefs talk to their suppliers to find out what's available. Often, this translates as the local farmer dropping by the kitchen for a cup of coffee and a natter. "Often they're all sitting around in the kitchen chatting,

on." She has been here since 2002 and turned the Mill from a 'Harvester-style' pub into a smart restaurant with rooms. The awards have flowed steadily but Liz has further challenges in her sights. "I'm thinking about turning one of the outbuildings into a microbrewery," she says. "And if I could buy some more land near the Mill, I could put in some treehouses. Proper, sustainable ones."

The Mill has a growing reputation for its food. "We are not pretentious and don't throw things on the plate. We quite like 'towers' and 'drizzles' but hate 'foams' and 'smudges'. Everything is there for a reason."

Liz and her chefs have become more fanatical about where their food comes from. "Before, we used to order whatever our butcher and greengrocer had," Liz admits.

or customers drop by with quinces, damsons or veg; one chap in the village supplies us with cucumbers and tomatoes in the summer and gets free lunches in winter."

The menu takes well-known classics and gives a little twist: layers of smoked chicken on an apple blini, for example, twice-baked Isle of White blue cheese soufflé with pickled walnuts or fillet of sea bass with oriental noodles. They do bar food, too, and The Mill draws huge numbers for Sunday lunch; people drive up to an hour to eat here and many week-enders come from London.

The low-ceilinged, beamed restaurant has a carefully relaxed elegance with honey-coloured wood panelling, an eclectic mix of polished tables, splashes of raspberry in curtains and cushions, and carved Javanese day-beds

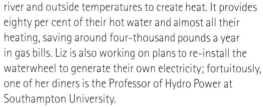

cleverly recycled as bench seats. Given even the merest hint of sunshine, you should bag a table on the riverside terrace where you will still find highly polished glasses and linen napkins and maybe see kingfishers and herons. The cosy bar, insists Liz, is genuinely used as a local.

Although she has a big team of twenty-seven full-time staff, Liz is very much hands-on, taking orders, talking through the menu and catching up on news with the regulars. One of her team has been with her for nineteen years and her gardener started as a waitress eighteen years ago; Terri, the manager, has been with her

river and outside temperatures to create heat. It provides eighty per cent of their hot water and almost all their heating, saving around four-thousand pounds a year in gas bills. Liz is also working on plans to re-install the waterwheel to generate their own electricity; fortuitously, one of her diners is the Professor of Hydro Power at Southampton University.

They have a chemical-free septic tank and a rubbish compactor; paper is recycled then shredded for 'duck bedding' for Crispie, a rescued duckling; menus are re-used as notepads. Instead of hothouse flowers, she

for thirteen years; Maggie used to be a customer and now runs the front bar and does the breakfasts. "The greatest compliment anyone can pay me is to say what friendly caring staff I have," says Liz. She recently arranged for one of her young waiters, who had no qualifications but huge enthusiasm, to spend several months working in an Australian vineyard to increase his wine knowledge.

The Mill is used for charity fundraising lunches, musical evenings and casino nights as well as for art and sculpture exhibitions by local artists. Many who come are fascinated to learn of the environmental measures Liz has taken. For example, she has installed a heat exchanger in the river, a clever system of pipes that "works like a reverse refrigerator", utilising the difference between the

commissioned a local sculptor to make table decorations from recycled cutlery and kitchen equipment. "Being eco-friendly becomes a way of life," she says but asserts that she isn't the hearty outdoors type. "I'm a businesswoman and I love heels and make-up so if I can do it anyone can."

The Mill at Gordleton

Evening main courses £14.95–£24.95
Beat meal deal: 2-course midweek lunch £12.50
No food on Christmas Day
Nearest train: Brockenhurst

The Thomas Lord

West Meon Petersfield
Hampshire GU32 1LN
01730 829244 www.thethomaslord.co.uk

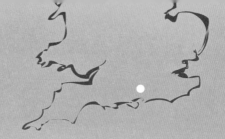

The Thomas Lord pub does not serve orange juice. And don't expect Tabasco with your Bloody Mary, parmesan on your pasta or lemon with your fish. Instead there will be local Hill Farm apple juice, Fireball hot sauce, Lyburn farmhouse cheese and lemon thyme butter. Frustrated by the ubiquitous slogan "local and seasonal wherever possible", David Thomas and Richard Taylor set out to prove it was always possible.

"Pubs have become like high streets – identical everywhere. People walk in expecting peas and carrots with their roast whatever the season. But we won't be swayed. It's perfectly possible to eat local all year round. Ninety-seven percent of our food is from Hampshire, and if you'll forgive us the black pepper, it's an all-British kitchen."

This doesn't mean going without variety: ten or more vegetables adorn Sunday roasts. Even in winter they rainbow around the lovely handmade plates – emerald broccoli, purple carrots, pink Chioggia beetroots, black cabbage, red cabbage, earthy bean sprouts, creamy cauliflower, golden parsnips – and put the usual and unseasonal pub trios to shame.

David and Richard were so sick of the depressing microwaved meals at their village local, that when the lease came up they put their money where their mouths were. With the help of fellow locals they stripped away the dated décor to reveal the inn's natural charm.

The pub is named after the founder of Lord's cricket ground (who lived in the village), which may help explain the stuffed squirrels, stoats and weasels playing cricket above the bar. Parquet flooring, chipped panelling, worn leather sofas and perching stools in front of fireplaces avoid any hint of gastropub pretension. Food-lovers, the muddy booted and dogs are all welcome.

After a string of problematic chefs – one was sacked for ordering imported sweet potatoes – Gareth Longhurst arrived and fell in love. "It's been brilliant getting to know Hampshire producers personally. I had to trade in my VW Golf for a Land Rover to collect supplies." From his banter-filled kitchen comes a daily changing modern British menu which is refreshingly short.

Gareth had to give up lemons, capers, chocolate, vanilla, spices and other ingredients he'd taken for granted. Instead he raids Richard's potager – chocolate or pineapple mint, orange or lemon thyme, anise hyssop. Panna cotta scented with lemon verbena fools diners into thinking they've rumbled a culinary transgression. And pears poached in Hampshire red wine burst with flavour despite lacking the usual cinnamon and cloves.

"One cook missed making curry, so we hacked into every curry plant in the garden. It tasted fantastic and sold out. We're waiting for the plants to grow back so we can have another!" says David, who is growing winter savory for its seed – a possible alternative to imported black pepper. Meanwhile Gareth experiments with local squirrel, delicious when potted with South Downs butter.

Fifth generation farmer Richard Jones provides organic meat and poultry: Longhorn beef faggots with mash; pork and herb sausages with cider cream; chicken terrine with carrot chutney. Wonderful staff know exactly who reared the meat on your plate.

David's biggest battle is seafood. "We want Marine Stewardship Council approved sustainable fish from local waters, but fishmongers just don't get it." He does trust family-run Portland Shellfish in Dorset and is always on the look out for traceable tagged line-caught bass. "It's what we expect for meat, so why not fish?"

In summer the outdoor brick oven is fired up for pizzas served on wooden rounds. Richard's inquisitive quails look on from the coop, and keep the kitchen in eggs. Those from the hens are sold on the bar, labelled with their creator's names. Past the hurdle fence, a table for two nests in the potager amid grape vines and cooks scurrying in and out to pick salad leaves, edible flowers and soft fruits moments before they are served.

Bar policy is relaxed to accommodate gin and tonics with lemon, whiskies, rums and wines from around the world. "As a tied house it's difficult to be local.

We persuaded them to let us stock only Hampshire ales and we're working on the lagers." House wines are English, teas from Tregothnan Estate in Cornwall, the first to be grown in England, and fairtrade coffee is supplied by Mozzo in Southampton.

At the far end of the bar hides a cosy semi-private dining room, encased in shelves of second-hand books sold in aid of local projects – primary school sports facilities, church clock, village hall. David's previous background in theatre has inspired live performances here and more projects are planned: a B&B, fringe theatre and an artisan bakery at David and Richard's second pub, the Red Lion up the road. "That's freehold, so be prepared for madness," he laughs.

The Thomas Lord

Evening main courses £11–£18
Members of 'Hampshire Fare'
Closed on Monday
Nearest train: Petersfield

The Wellington Arms

Baughurst Road Baughurst
Hampshire RG26 5LP 0118 982 0110
www.thewellingtonarms.com

Jason King, an energetic Australian, is delighted that British caterers are becoming more adept at utilising their local, seasonal produce. "In Australia we have always taken care to know all our ingredients' provenance and cooked seasonally, using produce at its freshest and least expensive. We'd never serve parsnips in summer or asparagus in winter. This awareness was around there long before the current interest here, so it's something that comes naturally to us. We even started keeping bees when a customer challenged our use of 'local' honey because it was made ten miles away!"

Jason and Simon Page are joint owners of The Wellington Arms, which they bought together in 2005.

chestnut dumplings; twice-baked Marksbury cheddar soufflé – a favourite of the keen regulars. Occasional special dinners indulge Jason's love of North African, Middle Eastern and south-east Asian flavours. Moroccan chicken and apricot stew spiced with his own ras-al-hanout; falafels with harissa and zhoug paste. Australian Murray River pink salt (coloured naturally by minerals) is one of several links to his homeland.

Out in the garden plum trees cast dappled shade over summertime tables. In the raised beds and polytunnel grow squashes, potatoes, cabbages, tomatoes and salad leaves. Herbs tumble from pots by the kitchen door. "I've always grown my own veg and enjoy getting out into the garden between shifts. In the summer most of our

Jason has twenty years experience working for some of the world's best chefs and his considerable international experience gives some unique twists to their ever-changing menu.

Influenced entirely by what's in season as well as what's growing in their own garden, they always serve new and inventive dishes alongside enduring favourites. Local rabbit and wood pigeon terrine with a chutney of Angela's apples; wild venison stew with shallots and

vegetables come from the garden," says Jason. One of his specialities is crispy fried pumpkin flowers stuffed with ricotta, parmesan and lemon zest. Bagfuls of quinces, plums, apples and damsons are also brought by the neighbours to be magicked into chutneys and jams. Four Tamworth pigs live happily in the woods behind, on land that is rented in return for a supply of ham, and in the adjoining paddock there are one hundred and fifty rare-breed Welsummer, Maran and Cream Legbar

chickens. "Ham, egg and chips couldn't be better: home-cured ham, a fried egg from our hens and potatoes we grew, cut and fried." Their pork belly is slow-roasted and served with sticky red cabbage and tart damsons.

Surrounded by pastures and woods and neighbours who enjoy a shoot, The Wellington doesn't want for game. "Many loyal customers arrive with surplus pheasants, rabbits, geese, ducks and crayfish happy to see them put to good use. It can be chaotic out the back with fur and feathers everywhere, but it's a great chance for the team to learn new skills. I'm passionate about passing on my knowledge, and I'm really proud of some of our trainees – teenagers who couldn't even peel an onion when they started, but who are now reaching an extremely high

flowers look perfect and we're completely ready." Personal touches fill the pub's dining room: Simon's mum's hand knitted tea-cosies, Jason's preserves and hens' eggs for sale on the bar, two Norfolk terriers padding between the eight tables. Simon pots up bulbs in winter to ensure a continuous supply of hyacinths and miniature daffodils for table decorations in spring.

It's said that good things come in small packages but Simon and Jason feel the need to spread out: the dilapidated oak-framed barn is earmarked for development into guestrooms and extra dining. "We want to leave space in the bar for additional drinkers or late-callers who fancy just cheese or pudding with a glass of wine. Those people are as important to us as the diners."

standard." One local lad, Dan, impressed Jason so much with his regular visits and offerings of trout that they took him on in the kitchen. His trout is potted with shallots, chilli, lemon zest and dill or tea-smoked by Dan himself.

It's a relaxed atmosphere and having supper feels more like eating in with good friends than 'going out'. That said, you generally have to book well in advance to get a table here. Simon, who runs front of house says, "I love getting ready for service, when the tables are set, candles lit, the

The Wellington Arms

Evening main courses £10–£17.50
Monday–Friday 2-/3-course lunch £15/£18
No food on Sunday night
Nearest train: Basingstoke

The Burpham Brasserie

Burpham Arundel
Sussex BN18 9RJ 01903 882160
www.burphamcountryhouse.com

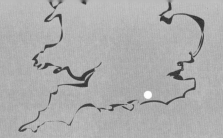

"Fine British cooking is often a term used about my cooking, but I'm not sure what defines it. Serving purely 'British' food would be very difficult. It's an amalgamation of influences from wherever we've been: dates and quinces brought back from Turkey during the Crusades, potatoes and tomatoes from the Americas, chutneys and spices from India.

"Truly indigenous British cuisine would be incredibly dull. The Romans were so disgusted by what they found here – basically grain, mutton, leeks and turnips – they introduced most of the vegetables we eat today, including onions, carrots and cabbages. Overseas influences have characterised most centuries of British food since then."

Steve Penticost is passionate about food. He and wife

fusion of bistro simplicity and iconic British dishes."

While eighty per cent of produce served at The Burpham Brasserie is sourced locally, Steve is not religious about the rest. "Beef, for example, is not a big thing here in West Sussex - lamb dominates - but when I use it I'll buy the best-tasting aged beef from my local butcher, which may come from Scotland or Devon. I also buy fabulous free-range chicken and duck from a family farm in Gascony in France, which is as close to here as northern Scotland. French farms have retained fantastic traditional poultry rearing skills."

As signed-up members of the 'Simply Ask' campaign (www.simplyask.org.uk), the Penticosts only use free-range chicken - eggs will soon come from their own hens

Jackie retired from successful business careers to run Burpham (pronounced Bur-fum) that was built as a hunting lodge in 1720 and is now a small country hotel.

"I am always traveling to France and Europe and finding, even in the smallest village, a little bistro or café serving simple but great home cooked food," says Steve. "Our style is slightly more elegant than that, but is a

– and encourage guests to check suppliers elsewhere. "People have come to expect whatever whenever, and at cheap prices. Chicken was once expensive and a treat, but horrific battery production methods have changed that."

Winter sees Steve roasting partridge to serve with savoy cabbage and earthy lentils or making game terrine and homemade piccalilli; spring sees roast rump of local

lamb with home-grown new potatoes and rosemary jus and the arrival of locally grown asparagus. In summer, grilled local black bream or sea bass with samphire risotto and classic summer pudding appear on the menu; in autumn, Old Spot pork with apricot and sage stuffing.

The Penticosts take equal pleasure in supporting artisan producers and growing their own heritage carrots, salad leaves and herbs.

Before and after dinner in the popular brasserie, guests congregate in the lounge, help themselves from the honesty bar, say hello to 'Fat Lucy' the languorous resident cat and slip into easy conversation.

From October until February Burpham specialises in locally caught game: wood pigeon with sweet potato rösti and blackberry jus; pheasant with wild mushrooms and sloe gravy; venison haunch with celeriac gratin.

"Pheasants – also introduced by the Romans – are now bred in their thousands and released into the wild a few months before shooting begins. It's big business around here and employs hundreds of people," explains Steve, "and the estates look after the countryside year-round, to the benefit of walkers and wildlife." For seafood Steve uses local suppliers, buying from day-boats, to provide a wide variety of sustainable fish: Pollack, bream, grey mullet, gurnard and wild sea bass, together with flat fish such as lemon and Dover soles. Excellent crab and lobster come from nearby Selsey Bill.

Southdown lamb is thought by many to be the best lamb in England thanks to the herby diet they enjoy on the chalk downs turf. "You can taste the sweet grass and herbs," says Steve, "and lamb has become a customers' favourite. The satisfying thing is that it's naturally available all year. In winter we slow cook 'hogget', lamb that is over a year old, in cinnamon, ginger, saffron and dried fruit for a Moroccan-style stew. In medieval England they often cooked meat with spices and fruit, so even this is not such a foreign dish," says Steve.

The Burpham Brasserie

Evening main courses £13–£19
Nov–Jan food only on Friday and Saturday eves.
Feb–Oct, no food Sunday or Monday
Nearest train: Arundel

Cocoa Loco

The Chocolate Barn Hill House Farm
West Grinstead Sussex RH13 8LG
01403 865687 www.cocoaloco.co.uk

Since starting her cottage industry of all things chocolate in 2005, Sarah Payne has never tired of "testing" the organic chocolate bars, buttons, truffles, brownies and cookies she makes everyday in the Chocolate Barn.

"Sarah started by making brownies when she was on maternity leave," says husband Rory "and her brownies were so popular with her friends that she started selling them on eBay. They sold brilliantly, and soon the house was overflowing with sacks of flour and cocoa. I was constantly chased out of the kitchen while she pulled tray after tray out of the Aga."

So Rory took a giant leap of faith and resigned from his IT job to help. He built a mini chocolate factory in the garden, but still Sarah only had space to make thirty bars of chocolate at a time. A nearby ice cream factory, built inside an old milking shed, provided the solution, and Dawn Stimpson joined the team as master chocolatier. They now sell online through their website and at independent shops and cafés.

While Sarah bakes, Dawn dips candied peel and nuts in molten chocolate and crafts bars, some studded with hazelnuts and cocoa nibs, others scented with rose geranium or orange oil. Truffle-making usually causes hysterics – a fiddly process requiring two pairs of hands. The best-seller is a bar spiced with chilli, a favourite pairing for chocolate since Mayans whisked up the first cups of hot chocolate. These bars use Nagas, the hottest peppers known to man.

Their chocolate has always been organic and they've not wavered during the recession. "Either you care about the environment or you don't. There's no half-way house," says Rory. "Naturally, cacao trees grow on mountainsides in gaps in the rainforest's canopy, and like specific conditions. Mass production drives the growth of monocultures, planted on thin soils requiring gallons of artificial fertilisers and pesticides, making it one of the most chemically intensive crops in the world. The ecosystem and the workers are normal."

The Paynes' chocolate is made from beans grown by a cooperative of small-scale farmers in the Dominican Republic that grows cacao trees without sprays and in harmony with the forest. Fat pods are hacked open to extract sweet-sour white pulp and beans, which are fermented – essential for developing chocolate's distinctive flavour – and sun-dried. A Belgian company roasts and grinds the beans, then mixes in extra cocoa butter, sugar and vanilla.

Dawn then tempers the chocolate through careful melting, temperature control and moulding to create perfectly shiny, hard and snappable confections. It is both science and art form.

"Our dark chocolate is seventy-three per cent cocoa solids, made only with cocoa butter, sugar and vanilla. Industrially produced dark chocolate often contains only forty per cent cocoa solids; milk chocolate is only half that and the rest is bulking agents such as hydrogenated vegetable fat, palm oil, flour, extra sugar or whatever's cheapest on the global market."

The Paynes make sure they know the provenance of each ingredient and trust its supplier. All are organic (except Naga chillies, for which certification is unavailable), and many are fairtrade. It took Sarah three years to find candied orange peel she liked, organic fairtrade desiccated coconut proves elusive, and some fairtrade ingredients require minimum orders that are way beyond Cocoa Loco's capacity.

Their packaging is recycled, recyclable and printed with water-soluble inks. Wrappers that look like plastic are in fact made from biodegradable cellulose and maize, not petroleum. Rory recycles religiously, leaving just one household bin of rubbish from the business per week.

The Paynes do not want to sell their chocolates to the big supermarkets. "As a small business they would soon have us over a barrel, financially and in terms of the pressure they would put on us. Also, many of our small customers don't want to stock products available in major supermarkets, and we do not want to trade with businesses where the big driver is shareholder return at the expense of treating suppliers fairly."

So Rory and Sarah continue happily at their own pace. They experiment constantly with new pairings: tomato, black pepper, even goat's cheese. Their current favourite creation is whole chocolate-coated chillies.

"*Either you care about the environment or you don't. There's no half-way house*"

The Griffin Inn

Fletching Uckfield
Sussex TN22 3SS 01825 722890
www.thegriffininn.co.uk

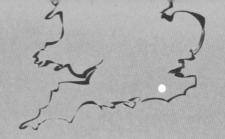

When a bowl of scampi and chips was considered new and exciting, Bridget Pullan was bringing Elizabeth David's recipes to East Sussex. From her kitchen at the Griffin Inn, which she bought in 1977, shone a light at the dawning of Britain's food revolution; long before the term 'gastropub' was invented, Bridget was dousing with extra virgin olive oil, crushing garlic and grating Parmesan.

Today, son James oversees the daily changing Italian and Spanish-influenced menu. Meals in the white tableclothed dining room start with house-made focaccia and peppery Sicilian olive oil, and might continue with fried goat's cheese-stuffed courgette flowers, roast bream with chickpeas, chorizo and olives, and lemon balm panna cotta. The chalked bar menu, with moules marinière, chargrilled ribeye steak and fish and chips, satisfies a crowd wanting something more casual in the oak-panelled front room.

"Our customers are a great mix of villagers, people from London and continentals. And you might find yourself sitting next to the person who reared your steak or picked your greens." The Griffin is a million miles from the freezer-to-fryer era of pub dining, but some things never change – this sixteenth-century inn has poured beer for half a millennium without a break.

James convinced neighbours Ian and Nicola Setford to expand their vegetable plot and reserve it entirely for the Griffin. The Setfords now enjoy a guaranteed market, while the pub gets regular deliveries of freshly plucked broad beans, ruby chard, artichokes, courgette flowers, tomatoes and herbs of all kinds – up to eighty per cent of the kitchen's needs.

"We used to source fish from Newhaven and Billingsgate. Then I stumbled across Paul Hodges, who fishes from his catamaran, and persuaded him to drive up from Rye twice a week by committing to buy his whole day's catch. We never knew what we'd get, so cooks were kept on their toes! It's been so successful he now comes daily and supplies other nearby restaurants."

Grilled line-caught sea bass is paired with olive tapenade and salsa verde; pan-fried bream with mussel stew and zesty gremolata; seared dived Rye Bay scallops with rosemary and sweet potato; crab with linguine, chilli and capers. "It amazes me how our chefs constantly devise new dishes: one just returned from Sicily with a recipe for butterflied sardines stuffed with pine nuts, raisins and breadcrumbs."

Meat and game come from surrounding farms and local butchers, including Romney salt marsh lamb, which "seasons itself from inside out". The wine list, featuring many from lesser-known Italian producers, includes two from Sussex: sparkling whites from Breaky Bottom and Ridgeview wineries, which benefit from the area's

geological similarities to Champagne. Real ales include Harveys of Lewes and Hepworth's Sussex.

Summer weekends see the firing of the giant grill and brick oven for al fresco food theatre. Fish glisten in ice on marble trays and a cocktail bar of anointments are on hand for the chef: garlic, chilli and lime; paprika and fennel oil; herb butters and pestos. Hundreds flock for spit-roasted chickens, rosemary-studded legs of lamb, slow-roasted pork belly and lobsters from the apple wood and hickory perfumed oven. "Everyone lazes around enjoying jazz bands and bucolic views – like Woodstock but with better food," says James.

Autumn game may come roasted with pomegranate molasses, or juniper jus. "We take whole animals from nearby shoots, deal with fur and feathers ourselves, then make a point of using all the meat, ending up with stews and sausages," says James, who also encourages cooks to forage mushrooms – boletus, chanterelles, chicken of the woods and ink caps – for autumnal risottos and bruschette.

In winter, five open fireplaces fuelled with coppiced wood, create a cosy atmosphere. Sunday lunchers linger late, often until dusk. "We only ever have one sitting. How can anyone enjoy their meal if they feel a crowd breathing down their neck?"

Late spring is James's favourite season, when village cricket resumes and the pub's three teams pile in for post-match beers on the sunset-facing terrace, delighting tourists.

"Americans have a clear-cut image of a picture-postcard English village pub. We tick all those boxes, and then surprise them with excellent food and service. The last thirty years has seen British dining make an amazing one hundred-and-eighty degree turn-around. We've overtaken France!"

The Griffin Inn

Evening main courses £9–£20
Best meal deal: 2-course lunch, £13.50
Lunch and dinner served everyday
Nearest train: Haywards Heath

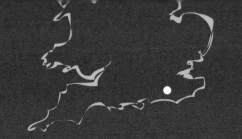

"My number one concern about food is that my family can eat without fear of contamination. I want to be able to eat a carrot as it comes, without having to peel off the skin and throw it away." Martin Tebbut is deadly serious about the state of food in Britain, and passionate about his mission to give Sussex folk a healthy alternative to supermarkets.

Martin took over the Boathouse farm in 1988 when its shop was a small shed with an honesty box by the side of the A26. They have seen a steady rise in custom, despite the recession. "People are questioning where their food comes from. We get a lot of mums and people who've had health problems and want unadulterated foods." Martin suspects food processing is the cause of many modern health issues. "In the history of food, the last fifty years have seen the introduction of thousands of new substances. None of us knows their impact, individually or as a cocktail. Each step of processing doubles a food's value for the manufacturer but halves its nutrition. I don't think any supermarket food is good food. Even if it once was, it isn't by the time it reaches the shelf."

It's not just our health that fuels Martin's passion, but also the planet's. Living in New Mexico among native American Indians for several years had a profound impact on his values and he learned to appreciate nature's beauty and complexity. He became interested in the Gaia and Chaos theories that maintain that seemingly random, complex systems are understandable patterns of connections with cascading repercussions. "We are

stewards of the Earth," says Martin, "I want to eat food that's been produced with respect for nature and soil."

That so many people don't understand the fragility of natural resources depresses and enrages him. "I've shouted at customers, and probably lost a few as a result. If someone complains about paying £1.50 for a lettuce, I say, do you know the price of houses round here? They have money, they just don't want to pay the real cost of food. I worry that many children will grow up with taste memories of industrially produced food and will never long for real food."

But Martin's optimism shines through: "Over the next fifty years food and water scarcity are going to be huge issues, so people will start to think harder - even if they are doing so purely because they are forced into it."

The shop is renowned for its organic meats. "Supermarket meat isn't hung properly and isn't cut properly. There's no respect for the animal," says Martin. "People buy packets not real meat, and supermarkets do all they can to obscure the cost per kilogram, so it's almost impossible to compare. Here we use everything – for example, we use the trotters to make the jelly for my chef Phil's delicious pork pies. Anything thrown away is an insult to the animal you've killed."

Their beef, mutton and lamb, whether from their own or local farms, is from animals fed predominantly on grass. "It gives a completely different taste. It's much better for your health; and the composition of the fat is very different."

Martin makes award-winning sausages flavoured with fennel, basil, garlic and cheese. Having taught himself how to cure and smoke, he sells his own bacon, collar and gammon and uses no nitrites or nitrates and experiments with salami and chorizo.

Martin is perhaps most proud of his wife Sally's partnership with Thames Reach Bondway, a London charity that supports homeless people. Every week during summer, ten to fifteen volunteers spend the day helping Sally plant, weed and harvest. The Tebbuts believe in the transformative power of working with nature and seeing the results of your graft. "We have seen people transform from addicts to people who have really got it together and who hold down a job." One of Channel 4's Secret Millionaires agreed their work was inspirational and made a donation to the project.

The Tebbuts have a pub nearby, the Halfway House with food skilfully prepared by their chef Phil. This is where you will find those pork pies. There are plans to open a café, too, and Martin's on the lookout for "a banker with a bonus burning a hole in his pocket, who wants to invest in something honest and sustainable" to help finance a bigger and better shop building.

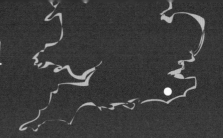

David and Tamzin Whittingham were running a small town bookshop in the Cotswolds when dreams of living on the land formed in their minds. Keen to find a large plot to buy, they headed for the East Sussex countryside, where they found Hidden Spring – a smallholding with a vineyard. "We had imagined running a campsite and doing a little food production, but it ended up the other way round. We've always liked knowing where our food came from. Now we produce much of it ourselves," says David.

Visitors are welcome to book camping and caravan sites, which overlook vines and orchards, and there are two Mongolian yurts. Look out for occasional willow-weaving workshops, too. "We love people staying. Sharing our smallholding life is what it's all about."

David's first ambition was to drastically reduce the

which are available for campsite guests to taste and buy.

The apple and pear orchards are fully organic. David presses Ida Reds, Coxes, Katies, Russets, Jonagolds and Bramleys into single variety juices. "I simply pasteurise it and nothing is added." Extras and windfalls end up in Tamzin's jellies and chutneys.

Some fruit is saved for cider-making. "Big brand advertising has made cider fashionable and it's no longer regarded as just a hangover-inducing festival drink," says David. Mass-produced cider is usually made from concentrate and additives, but Hidden Spring's is simply pressed apple and pear juices fermented by naturally occurring yeasts. "It tastes very much like the fruit, without that 'scrumpiness.'"

Traditional and rare breed sheep graze orchards and pastures – blotchy Jacobs and Balwens, black with a

amounts of weed-killers and pesticides used in the growing of the grapes. "Having children focused the mind: if the chemicals were too dangerous for them to be around and if you needed to not touch the vines after spraying, I figured there was something wrong."

Reichensteiner, Faber, Pinot Noir and Dunkelfelder vines yield enough fruit to produce around two thousand bottles of wine a year. Grapes go to Roy Cook at Sedlescombe Organic Vineyard (see overleaf), who returns them as light, summery easy-drinking wines,

badger-like white flash down the face, white socks and tails that look half-dipped in white paint. Rapidly multiplying chickens – Ixworths, Araucanas, Crested Legbars and Welsummers – range free, self-medicating on Tamzin's herbs, and give beautiful white, blue and brown eggs. "We try to integrate animals with the whole system," explains David.

To complement their traditional breeds, they grow heirloom vegetables. Tamzin is particularly proud of her beans – purple Blauhilde and climbing Trail of Tears, said

to be saved from the forced relocation of seventeen thousand Cherokees in 1838. She also allows squashes free-rein over the garden – football-sized Rondo di Nizza, blue-grey Twonga, stripy Sweet Lightning, intensely orange Uchiki Kuri.

"You can't save F1-hybrid seeds as they do not come up true to the parent plant, so you have to buy another pack, which is good for the seed selling industry. It's criminal that so many old varieties – which are cut-and-come-again or whose seeds come up true year after year – are being sidelined by F1-hybrids," says David. The Whittinghams source mainly from Kate McEvoy and Ben Gabel's Real Seed Catalogue; Kate and Ben are champions of non-hybrid rare and unusual varieties.

The family's diet has changed and they eat less meat and more vegetables. "But we're by no mean vegetarian.

We just stretch a chicken out to three or four meals because we saw what went into its life. Some people are horrified that we kill our own chickens, but is getting it in plastic packets from the supermarket better? It's incredibly important that the next generation knows where their food comes from."

Seeing how much food they can produce without ripping up great swathes of countryside fascinates David and Tamzin. "When Russia abandoned Cuba and the oil supply ran dry, the large state Cuban farms collapsed and thousands of people acquired small plots," says David. "They grow more leaves and fewer grains; city dwellers keep chickens on roofs and many grow their own vegetables. Now Cuba is much more self-sufficient in food. We may need to do something similar here in the UK and create a new approach to our food supply."

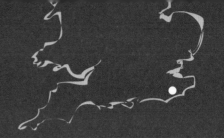

Sedlescombe Vineyard

Cripp's Corner Sedlescombe Robertsbridge
Sussex TN32 5SA 01580 830715
www.englishorganicwine.co.uk

North of Battle, deep in '1066 country', lies Britain's oldest organic vineyard. Roy Cook makes award-winning wines at Sedlescombe without using the synthetic fertilisers, pesticides, herbicides or processing aids common to conventional wine-making. "Organic wine has to start with healthy vines so I put energy into producing exceptional grapes; conventional producers can cover up all kinds of problems with additives."

In 1974 Roy inherited ten acres when self-sufficiency was all the rage. "I tried to live off the land but soon realised I couldn't make matchsticks, saucepans and clothes, so needed an income." Already familiar with the basics of fermentation and of making pea-pod, beetroot and elderberry wines, Roy hit on the idea of viticulture.

In fact at that time there was something of a wine-

vineyard to twenty-two acres. Germanic varieties - Reichensteiner, Bacchus, Rivaner (aka Muller Thurgau), Regent and Solaris - appreciate England's cool climate. From Germany too came Irma, his partner. "It must have been my pea-pod wine that impressed her and she came to live with me in my caravan!"

Wines, as well as cider, fruit wines, juices (below, far right) and liqueurs are available in the shop, at farmers' markets, on-line and from several merchants. Roy leads groups of visitors through the vineyard and ancient woodland before finishing with a look at the cider- and wine-making processes and tastings.

Irma set up a very popular Rentavine scheme. Members receive discounted wines, first option on speciality small batches, and opportunities to learn the craft of viticulture from Roy through his regular

making revival taking place in southern England. Says Roy, "My land was perfect, being south-facing and sheltered. I helped out on a nearby vineyard, brought back cuttings and planted them." Five years later, a roadside sign advertised Roy's first vintage. "People ventured in and liked what they tasted. That was a fantastic moment."

Today, those original plants - the oldest organic vines in Britain - are flourishing, and Roy has expanded his

newsletters. They can also have their own wine labels created and can help in the vineyard and attend special tours and tastings. "The pleasure comes from this being wine with a story, not something anonymous from the supermarket," says Roy.

Roy is especially proud of his red: pleasingly peppery and fruity and unusually bold in colour and flavour for an English red. "The manual work we put into our vines in

place of chemical sprays has beneficial side-effects," he explains. "We remove leaves from around grape bunches to prevent disease and expose them to more sunshine. The result is a more intense, less acidic grape."

The white is reminiscent of German Rieslings, with its floral nose, notes of lemon zest and honey, and crisp finish. "It's a cracking wine and perfect as a summery aperitif," says Roy. A vibrantly hued dry rosé, sparkling white and sparkling rosé make up his range. None are dominated by alcohol: "We prefer around 11% – not the usual 13% – you can drink more without getting legless."

The butter mountains and wine lakes of the seventies sparked Roy's interest in organic growing. "It was ridiculous – all those polluting grow-faster chemicals producing all that surplus food." The stark contrast he witnessed between sterile vineyards treated with 'total

The result is a lusciously green, diverse habitat, alive with insects and birds and far from the endless pristine rows seen elsewhere.

Initially customers were confused by the organic label and shocked to hear Roy's tales of how systemic pesticides and fungicides are ingested when you drink non-organic wine. Roy just adds sulphur dioxide as a preservative but uses under half that permitted in conventional wines.

The international wine industry is oil-hungry. Aside from agrichemicals and machinery, there is the cooling of vast vats of wine and the transport of heavy bottles across the globe.

Unlike counterparts in Australia, Roy has an almost entirely local market, and no need for refrigeration. Wine lovers have little idea how grateful they may be

herbicide kill' and those blossoming with purple vetch and poppies convinced him. "The water that runs off crops treated this way pollutes groundwater which costs water companies millions and I suspect that's one reason our water bills have increased."

Instead of dousing soil with synthetic fertilisers, Roy spreads manure and plants rotations of winter rye, fodder radishes, clovers and lucernes between the rows of vines.

to trailblazers like Roy come the nemesis of peak oil.

It's easy to forget how English viticulture flourished after the Romans were here and how it continued to flourish until Henry VIII dissolved the monasteries and wiped out the monks' vines, cellars and know-how. Thanks to the skill and dedication of growers like Roy, Sedlescombe is now one of several hundred vineyards in England and the revival looks here to stay.

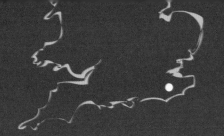

Hen on the Gate

Clayton Organic Farm
Newick Lane Mayfield Sussex TN20 6RE
01435 874852 www.henonthegate.com

"When you can pay £1.99 for a supermarket chicken you have to ask what kind of life it had. Cheap meat is rarely good for anybody: it's not good for the environment, really bad for the animal and not good for our health." Cathy Swingland and Will Sheffield aim to produce and sell the best possible quality meat without leaving behind a series of hidden costs. "All the meat in our shop – beef, lamb, mutton, pork and chicken – is raised on our farm. We pride ourselves on being transparent and anybody can come and watch any aspect of the production."

Cathy was brought up on a farm and when the fields

by her home in East Sussex came up for sale, she jumped at the chance to buy them. "The intensive arable farming was annihilating the wildlife but since farming it organically it has improved year on year. When I used to walk the footpaths here there was silence, but now it buzzes with bees, insects, birds and butterflies."

Will, who had grown up on a nearby turkey farm, came to manage Clayton Farm with Cathy a few years after she had taken over. "Cathy would say there were two organic conversions: the farm and me. I'd been conditioned to believe that all those sprays and antibiotics were essential."

Keen to share a taste of the magical childhood she had on her parents' farm, Cathy runs open days, school visits and children's arts workshops and hopes to impart an appreciation of the origins of honestly produced food. "Children learn much better when they are excited and can join in. They can collect eggs, watch the sheep shearing, see the Christmas turkeys strutting around outside." Many children, usually fussy eaters, arrive with packed lunches. "But after the fresh air, probably more than they'd usually get, they demolish large plates of our food and come back asking for more, discovering they do like meat after all!"

The Sussex cattle and Romney Cross sheep, both local breeds, are rotated round the fields, grazing freely. Pigs spend several months each summer enjoying the shade, pig nuts and acorns in the woods, and also save the farmhands some work by digging up and cleaning out the vegetable patches at the end of the growing season. "Sows often reject the huts we've provided and break off little branches in the woods to build their own nest to farrow in," says Will. "For me that epitomises organic farming as you are giving the animal freedom to exhibit its natural instincts."

"People don't always realise chickens like to graze fields too. The more grubs and grass they get, the tastier and deeper coloured their eggs will be." In the past a beautiful orange yolk would have signalled a genuinely free-range lifestyle with plenty of beta-carotenes from all the greenery eaten. "Now feed suppliers send conventional egg producers colour charts, like a paint chart, to choose the yolk colour." Small flocks mean no bullying or aggressive pecking order behaviour, so there is no need to de-beak the chickens, a common practice on intensive poultry farms.

The Swinglands made a decision to keep their retailing set-up small after a brief flirtation with a large shop a mile away. "Selling our produce outside the farm meant customers lost the connection." Now back at Clayton Farm, the Hen on the Gate shop is thriving, selling award-winning fresh and cured organic meats, free-range eggs, local vegetables, bread and cheeses and other products, plus organic chocolate and wine.

Smoked bacon, hams, salt beef and their own 'Sussex spiced beef' are dry-cured in-house. Sausages are made

with only 'real' ingredients and as a result were rejected by a supermarket for being 'too meaty'. "Tastes have changed," says Cathy, "and consumers have got used to artificial flavourings and the texture of cheap highly processed meat, rusk and gunge."

So can we really be persuaded to buy a twenty-pound chicken? "Ours are big, grown to at least twelve weeks rather than five, killed, dry-plucked and hung here. They have more flavour, and can provide four meals for a family of four: a roast, a cold dinner, a curry and a soup. But you need to do what our mums did - use every bit." Will and Cathy are adamant: we should be eating less meat, enjoy it more, and value it as special.

George and Dragon

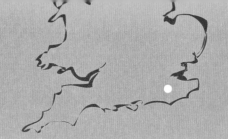

Speldhurst Hill Speldhurst
Tunbridge Wells Kent TN3 0NN
01892 863125 www.speldhurst.com

Julian Leefe-Griffiths likes to know where his food comes from, so some of it he shoots himself and the rest comes from a team of trusted local suppliers. "I love the simplicity of taking food straight from woods to the kitchen, missing out the industrial meat packing plants and polystyrene drip trays," says Julian, who shoots in the beautiful Ashdown Forest.

The pub's ethos of 'food from a farm, not a factory', is easy to maintain here on the Kent/Sussex border, among farms, orchards and exceptional producers. His chefs are spoiled for choice.

While savouring one particularly long and delicious lunch in an Italian village, a penny dropped: what made the meal so special was the connection between the countryside around and the food on the plate;

in trattorias all over Italy people expect their food to be local. "The ricotta was made in the village, malfatti hand-rolled in the kitchen, the wild boar had lived in the local woods, the chicken had been kept by a neighbour. I realised there were few such places in Britain, so set myself a challenge to do it here."

With its abundance of organic vegetables, soft and orchard fruits, seafood and game, Kent was an obvious place to choose to execute his vision. "It was remarkably easy. Within a month I had a long list of suppliers: oysters and samphire from Whitstable; fish landed at Hastings and Rye; smoked salmon and eel from Flimwell; organic poultry from Gill Wing five miles away; organic meat from Earl De La Warr six miles away."

The laws of supply and demand can work well if you are minding costs. Few want Gill Wing's duck hearts and chicken livers, but Julian takes bagfuls at a good price. He gets a bespoke service, too. "The Earl's Large Black pigs develop lean and fatty layers at different stages of growth, so I advise on their feeding to get perfectly succulent pork; our butcher ages each joint of beef differently for me – say thirty-two days for sirloin, thirty-seven for rump and forty-two for topside. You won't find that attention to detail in the supermarket."

The medieval half-timbered inn, one of the oldest in Britain, swiftly earned a reputation for good food and Michelin Bib Gourmand awards followed. Flagstones, fireplaces and blackened beams are the rustic backdrop for good gastropub grub. One of Julian's quarries gazes from the wall; foodies beat a path to the door; regulars prop up the bar like extras on a set; the cricket team piles in at weekends; bell-ringers call by every Tuesday.

Many dishes reflect Julian's love of simple Italian cooking: risotto with broad beans and peas, char-grilled lamb chops with salsa verde, roasted pancetta-wrapped pheasant breast with sage. "My wife Sarah was brought up in Italy, and we go on holidays that retrace her childhood travels. I always ask locals where they eat. That's how you find real food, made by real people."

Old standards are served at the George, too: steak and ale pie, beer battered haddock and chips and sausages and mash with onion gravy. The ploughman's is a generous pile of house-made bread and local cheeses with chutney,

pickled onions and lemon and onion seed relish. The fruity Indian Military chutney, from a one-hundred-year-old recipe, is so popular they sell it in jars, and they make rosemary focaccia, slow-risen pain levain and rye daily.

Julian's favourites are game dishes: terrine, pigeon with caramelised lentils, confit pheasant leg on cavolo nero. "I love slow-cooked comfort food, like hare or oxtail ragù on pappardelle." The meat is roasted one day, slowly braised the next, left to deepen its flavours overnight, then eaten on the third. It's a long process but the taste is all the better for it. Julian does occasional shifts in the kitchen and is fanatical about not wasting food: "We could all learn from our grandmothers, who used up every last bit of the animal."

Take his venison: chops are left with ten-inch rib bones, Flintstone style; loins rubbed with Szechuan pepper, seared and sliced for carpaccio; legs boned, rolled and roasted for Sunday lunch; tougher cuts braised for pies and stews; heart added to haggis; liver served on toast; and every last bit minced up for burgers. "Having ended its life myself, how could I not use it all?"

The kitchen used to receive deliveries of wood sorrel, sea purslane and other woodland, hedgerow and seashore treasures, until wild food became so trendy that their

forager, Fergus Drennan, was poached. Julian meanwhile takes off himself to Ashdown Forest for porcini, chanterelles, wood blewits, horse mushrooms and the occasional puffball, which he slices, dips in egg and then in parmesan-spiked breadcrumbs before frying and serving with pesto.

Julian finds it depressing that millions of Britons flock on auto-pilot to indistinguishable supermarkets once a week. "What moron came up with the idea of massive shops selling food that all tastes the same and that people end up throwing half of away? We've become so disconnected from the food chain, and turn a blind eye to the fact that there are warehouses of thousands of chickens and pigs jacked up on antibiotics, eating effluent and spreading disease."

George and Dragon

Evening main courses £9–£23
Best meal deal: Sunday lunch £14.50
No food Sunday evenings
Nearest train: Tunbridge Wells

Central & East England

Location

Key

 Alastair Sawday's Special Places to eat
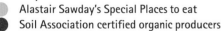 Soil Association certified organic producers

Map 4

Central & East
England

Growing Communities

Old Fire Station Stoke Newington
London N16 7NX 020 7502 7588
www.growingcommunities.org

Hidden from the road by townhouses and tucked into the corner of an East London park is a secret oasis where cheery volunteers tend a cornucopia of fruits, herbs, flowers and salad leaves, destined for a ground-breaking box scheme.

"We don't just want to supply beautiful organic fruit and vegetables, we want to reclaim control of food production and trade from agribusiness and supermarkets. We want to put the power back where it should be – with farmers and communities," says Julie Brown, the pioneering founder of Growing Communities.

The box scheme is the engine driving this wider mission. Profits from it helped launch London's first organically certified market garden, an apprenticeship scheme, and the UK's first fully organic farmers' market. And a community is emerging: of farmers, urban growers,

bananas travel from outside Europe. "We price food as affordably as possible, while allowing growers to make a living and work sustainably. During Britain's 'hungry gap' we import from Europe, but we never air freight or buy food grown in heated greenhouses. International trade is not a bad thing but it needs to be kept to a sensible scale."

With many of Kent's old orchards grubbed up, Julie has to import more fruit than she would like. "Only around five per cent of fruit eaten in Britain is grown in Britain. We source twenty per cent here, and we're working hard to increase that." As a result of the box scheme, brothers Chris and Iain Learmonth of Stocks Farm in Essex have significantly expanded their organic, traditional variety apple orchards.

Brightening each salad bag is a single edible flower – perhaps an orange marigold or violet pansy – the input of

land owners, artisan producers, cooks and consumers. "Living in London, I'd felt a disconnection from rural Britain and a sense of isolation and anonymity," says Julie. "I wanted to do something practical that built community and protected the environment."

Boxes are filled with produce grown here and within one-hundred miles of Hackney; only the fairtrade

head grower Ru Litherland, a self-confessed "vegetable nerd". Adapting permaculture principles, Ru has created lush urban gardens by planting the useful and the beautiful: banks of flowers delight volunteers and visitors and useful insects; certain flowers cleverly fix nitrogen in the soil; mustard, salsola, purslane, red orache, escarole and sorrel add an extra peppery note to the mixed salads.

Julie is piecing together a 'patchwork farm' – a series of organically certified microplots in residents' back gardens – and a larger suburban plot of land for Ru's apprentices. "It's great to see volunteers become apprentices, and apprentices start to contribute produce for the veg boxes."

Julie's favourite spot is the secluded Allens Gardens, which she resuscitated from urban decay. Fertile soil and fruit trees have replaced burnt out litter bins. Nineteenth-century architect Matthew Allen designed the housing there to give flat-owners access to balconies, roof gardens, communal greenhouses and even a croquet lawn; now, in the twenty-first century, Allen's vision of communality is re-emerging.

Locals flock to the Saturday Stoke Newington Farmers' market and children scamper between stalls

diverse cottage industries. There's Hatice Trugul's Turkish gözleme (traditional filled pancakes), chef Rafe Jaffrey's Indian pakoras and soups, Anne-Marie Ryan's lemon drizzle and coffee and walnut cakes, Anthony Ferguson's artisan chocolates, and the Market Chefs' demonstrations of seasonal dishes.

Perhaps nothing better illustrates the spirit of Growing Communities than the Big Food Swap where hundreds gathered to barter food they had grown, foraged or made themselves. It was like an inner city version of the Women's Institute. "People loved showing off their creations and discovering others," says Julie. "My children managed to trade some bay leaves from our garden all the way up to an enormous cake. Everybody wins. It was great fun to set up and we hope to do more."

Growing Communities, now a financially self-

as parents shop for biodynamic beef, rare breed pork and lamb, buffalo cheese, organic wines and more. Organiser Kerry Rankine explains that buying direct means fresher produce, fewer food miles and a fairer price for all. "Friendships form, so farmers are supported through good times and bad."

The market inspires and supports many culturally

sufficient business, is helping others set up similar ventures elsewhere. Julie has never felt more committed to community-led trade: "Our current global food system is incredibly unsustainable and extremely fragile. We've simply got to turn it round."

The Farmers' Market is held every Saturday at the William Patten School in Stoke Newington.

The Duke of Cambridge

30 St Peter's Street Islington
London N1 8JT 02073 593066
www.dukeorganic.co.uk

Remember the seventies...? When half the nation was laughing at Felicity Kendal struggling with chickens in 'The Good Life' and the other half was trying to make yogurt at home? At that time Geetie Singh was living on a self-sufficient commune at Birchwood Hall, Worcestershire, surrounded by the reality of organic vegetable growing. "It was an incredibly values-driven commune. Our life was based on thinking through the impact we would have on society. Everyone ate together and the conversation always turned to politics."

Most of Geetie's memories of her fourteen years growing up on the commune are food-related, yet she had no idea then that she would blaze a trail of her own and run her own restaurant.

She left the commune to train as an opera singer, but decided that working in London restaurants would be more fun. Geetie was shocked, however, by the outside world's disregard for the environment. "At Birchwood your ideals could become a reality; outside, it seemed, they couldn't. We were already buying fairtrade, recycling

and using wind power and I was appalled that qualified chefs did not cook seasonally or recycle." Geetie resolved to demonstrate that serving fabulous food did not mean compromising your environmental values.

She has set up three certified organic London gastropubs and won a string of awards. The Duke, tucked down a side-street in Islington, has been the flagship since it opened in 1998. "Most people were concerned with human health or cooking seasonally; my focus has always been on sustainability," says Geetie.

To comply with Geetie's uncompromising food sourcing restrictions - one-hundred per cent seasonal and organic - the large majority of ingredients come from London and the Home Counties, no special couriers are allowed and absolutely no air freight. Her team has built relationships with over sixty food and drink producers. Managing this is not easy, especially as many are tiny, may only supply one thing for a few weeks of the year, and are not geared up for the restaurant trade. But when the chefs want to lay their hands on treats such as apricots, aubergines and damsons, they put in the effort

and will wait around for very early or late deliveries.

Adrian Izzard is one of their producers: he grows vegetables year-round in unheated greenhouses and sells them at nearby Islington farmers' market, so the vegetables he supplies come with fewer food miles.

Then there's Todd Cameron-Clarke, who supplies the meat. His animals are reared on land mostly unsuited to cereal crops – so he is not displacing them. Todd also shoots – mostly game that is damaging to farms – bringing wild boar, rabbit and venison.

When he delivers the meat to London he brings their seafood order, too, from a Hastings' Marine Stewardship Council fishery. The pub adheres to the first ever fish policy approved by the Marine Conservation Society and offers only MSC fish. "The auditing is expensive," says Geetie, "but without having standards to adhere to it would be easy to make mistakes."

In the early days Geetie remembers their stance detracted from the quality of what they were serving. "I employ cooks for their professionalism and skill," explains Geetie, "but our press coverage made up stuff

about sandal-wearing veggie hippies and customers that didn't wear lipstick. They missed the point that what we were doing was largely for the planet's health, not ours."

Geetie's determination spreads beyond the pub doors: her staff work with cooks at a nearby primary school to revamp their menus and examine their food sourcing, so now two-hundred-and-fifty children enjoy a freshly made and mostly organic lunch. "The uptake of school meals has increased dramatically," she says. They also trained pupils of a local secondary to plan, prepare and serve their own food, restaurant-style. A third project with a nursery is planned, and Geetie intends to use these pilot projects as blueprints for other schools to follow.

Geetie is also active in several London-wide and national food strategy groups. She wants to see public institutions adopting sustainable food procurement policies; a network of small, independent producers, grouped into local co-operatives, supplying both them and restaurants; the government setting serious ethical business guidelines; the European Union properly protecting the label 'organic'. As it stands, any eatery can call itself 'organic' without certification. Geetie also fights to reduce farm pollution, water use, meat consumption and unsustainable fishing. As she puts it, "if businesses don't act responsibly with a moral code of conduct then God help us all. You can't expect people to do it voluntarily. We need legislation."

While many are disillusioned, Geetie is ever optimistic, having marvelled at how much has already changed since the days she was considered odd for using her own shopping bag. "We're absolutely capable of doing it. The organic movement came from individuals not governments and proves we can change the world through how we spend our money."

The Duke of Cambridge
Evening main courses £10.50–£21 Lunch and dinner served all week No food 3–6.30 each day Nearest train: Kings Cross

The Sun Inn

High Street Dedham Colchester
Essex CO7 6DF
01206 323351 www.thesuninndedham.com

"We look for quality, and so much happens to be organic, but we don't shout about it"

minimum percentages for freshly prepared, local and organic food, cooking and gardening clubs for children, and involvement of parents in supporting a culture of healthy food.

"School cooks see us and say 'oh no, here come the sacks of potatoes to peel!' But we're proud that schoolchildren are now drinking organic milk and eating local beef, free-range pork and fresh vegetables. Visits to Ashlyns are an important part of the programme. The kids adopt us as 'their farm', which means they're more likely to try the meat and vegetables our co-operative supplies," says Gary.

In the training kitchen, courses have expanded to include teenagers in care, disadvantaged families and drug and alcohol addicts. There are occasional cooking classes for members of the public, too. "We demonstrate that cooking from scratch can be quick, easy and cheaper than ready meals and take-aways. It's also about developing self-esteem, practising literacy and numeracy skills – for example by multiplying up recipe quantities – and having fun. Some teenagers have gone on to catering college," says Gary.

The farmers' co-op now also supplies hospitals in Epping and Braintree, and Ashlyns is offering catering services to improve food for patients, staff and visitors. "We're one of few such regional co-operatives supplying the public sector," says Gary.

"The beauty is that we also supply the private sector – vegetable box schemes, pubs and restaurants – and that helps to fill gaps in demand outside term time. So school children in Hackney are getting the same top quality ingredients as West End restaurants."

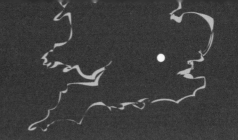

There has probably been a watermill here for a thousand years and its ownership has passed between Church, Crown and the Gorhambury Estate. In 1985 the Crown Estate sold Redbournbury Mill to Amanda and Julian James on condition they restored it. The Domesday survey recorded nearly 6,000 such watermills in southern England but during the second half of the nineteenth century shiploads of cheap American wheat arrived, following the repeal of the Corn Laws and the invention of steel roller mills. Village mills slowly disappeared.

Tenant miller Henry Hawkins produced the last flour here in the 1930s and his daughter Ivy was here in the old cowshed until the fifties, grinding animal feed. In 1993 flour spilled from the millstones for the first time in sixty years thanks to Amanda and Julian's restoration. Now people flock to watch Amanda's son Justin take the helm and, amid rhythmic clatters and clouds of flour, every Sunday afternoon visitors watch the mill and visit the museum or book a private tour, talk and tea.

Organic grain, from Hammonds End Farm two miles away in Harpenden, is hoisted to the top floor from where it slides into the eye of the 'runner' millstone, rotating a hair's breadth above the 'bedstone'. As grains radiate over the 'lands' and 'furrows' expertly carved on the French burr stone, they are ground into wholewheat flour. Some of the milled wheat is sieved to produce brown and white flours, semolina and bran. Justin also mills spelt, prized for its nutty full flavour, and rye.

Amanda and Justin are part of a water and windmill

revival: the Traditional Cornmillers' Guild is now thirty-strong. "There is a fascination with mills and locals help maintain machinery and sieve and bag flour, lead tours and run farmers' market stalls across Hertfordshire. Their payment? Bags of flour, freshly baked bread and endless cups of tea.

For many years the heavy iron waterwheel lay dormant as the river Ver dried up. "People are using far too much water," complains Amanda. "There's too much building, too many bathrooms." A 1932 Crossley oil engine, restored by Peter, a retired electrical engineer, has stood in. Water flow is increasing and Amanda is optimistic that most milling will be water-powered again. Following one of the picturesque valley walks, you can see how the river was diverted to achieve the necessary height of water, a massive feat of engineering.

"Our flour is natural, golden and unbleached. It's high in gluten, so ideal for bread-making," explains Amanda, who recommends storing flour in tins in a dry, cool place, and never in the fridge or in airtight plastic containers that make it sweat.

Some ends up in the hands of third generation baker Nick Anderson, who crafts artisan loaves in the old cowshed. "When his Stilton and raisin bread is cooking, the smell is to die for," says Amanda. "There is no comparison between a loaf made with our quality of grain, milling and baking and a supermarket loaf."

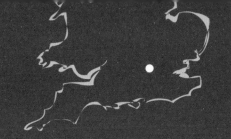

Waltham Place Farm
Church Hill White Waltham
Berkshire SL6 3JH
01628 825517 www.walthamplace.com

Strilli and husband Nicky, a South African of diamond fame, inherited Waltham Place twenty-five years ago and converted the large estate lock, stock and barrel to organic practices. Its one-hundred-and-seventy acres, just thirty-five miles west of London on the edge of a chalk belt, are a seamless blend of farmland, park and woodland.

"Every decision is guided by sound environmental, social and economic principals," says Vinnie McCann their project manager. Sixteen neighbours/colleagues run things collectively while Strilli is in South Africa and their views are respected not constrained. "Trying to impose a hierarchical system on the kind of free-thinking people attracted to work here would be impossible," says Vinnie.

There are few straight lines or conventional forms: yew hedges twist in whimsical, bulbous shapes. Apple

harvests. It draws people here again and again."

Strilli Oppenheimer describes herself as "a gardener of place" – following the natural ecology as it evolves rather than continually trimming to maintain a preconceived picture. "The garden is our legacy and represents our investment in the future."

Vegetables from the walled potager and market garden are sold here and at farmers' markets. Kohlrabi, heirloom tomatoes, cavolo nero, globe and Jerusalem artichokes were growing here long before their recent renaissance. Run on biodynamic principles – "way beyond organic" – crops are planted, weeded and harvested on specific days in the moon's cycle, following ebbs and flows in the earth's energy.

"These vegetables taste better," says Vinnie. "'Slow food' is as much about our approach in garden and field

trees, some nearly a century old, resist pruning, to the delight of woodpeckers and redwings. The animals defy farmland stereotypes.

"Waltham has that 'wow factor' you get when surrounded by the wild," enthuses Vinnie. "Everything – woodland, pastures, lake, gardens and parkland – forms one big living thing, bursting with births, deaths, wars and

as it is preparing and sharing meals." Vinnie recommends trialing a six-month diet of organic milk, eggs, vegetables and home-made bread to note the improvement in physical wellbeing.

Chef Adrian Foster has been on the estate for twenty-five years. When not making his organic jams, chutneys, cakes and breads for the shop and tearoom, he guides students through soup, bread and butter-making. Tearoom regulars love his fuchsia-pink rhubarb cordial and emerald nettle, sorrel and nasturtium leaf soups. "It's surprising how many other chefs invent dishes then have to manipulate ingredients to achieve them," says Vinnie.

At Waltham's 'Big Lunch', villagers were not offered the delicious Berkshire pork that had been roasted for twenty-four hours until they had looked at the 'Life of Brian' exhibition documenting the life of Brian the pig and his family. "How can you eat an animal you know?" asked one shocked woman. "How can you eat one you don't?" was the reply.

Education is Waltham's raison d'être. "Tours and classes aren't just walks in the countryside; people come here to learn," says Vinnie. "We want children to know

they will have an important role to play as consumers."

The large formal gardens were transformed by Dutch designer Henk Gerritsen, "The Jamie Oliver of the gardening world". Now, untainted by herbicides or pesticides, they flow in a natural, less tidy, manner. Some would say they challenge the very concept of a garden, joining forces with nature rather than dominating it.

Gardens are open under the National Garden Scheme on Wednesdays and Fridays from June to autumn and most visitors stop at the shop to buy robust varieties of their favourite vegetables which thrive without chemical intervention or rare breed meat. Head gardener Beatrice Krehl leads tours, seasonal walks take in spring bluebells and autumn apples, and 'Quiet Garden' events inspire spiritual contemplation.

"We want children to know they will have an important role to play as consumers"

The Sweet Olive

at The Chequers Inn Aston Tirrold
Didcot Oxfordshire OX11 9EN
01235 851272 www.sweet-olive.com

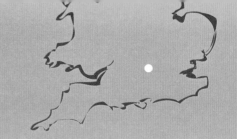

Pheasants are two-a-penny in this area yet even so Chef Olivier Bouet roasts the breasts, sautés the fillets with mushrooms, makes curry with the legs, and uses the bones for consommé. "Just because something's cheap, doesn't mean it should be wasted. These days we're surrounded by choice, so buy too much and then waste too much. Chefs are losing the skill of using the whole animal."

Olivier, from the Loire and from a family of chefs, trained under the Roux brothers and cooked his way around the world, then teamed up with fellow Frenchman Stephane Brun to take over the Chequers Inn; locals were delighted, and have learnt to be swift with their dinner reservations.

cricket team are regular drinkers, and Stephane will open specially on Sunday evenings after a match. Neighbours offer gluts of carrots, cucumbers, rhubarb and plums, encouraged by Olivier who can't bear to see them relegated to compost heaps. Fundraising events for local charities are frequent.

Transient treats are posted on the blackboard menu: fresh pot-caught Cornish crab and lobster, Scottish scallops with lime butter sauce, asparagus picked by Olivier. French cuisine – lamb's sweetbreads with mushrooms, rare beef onglet with red wine sauce, crème brulée – sits alongside Japanese tempura prawns, Caesar salad with homemade gravadlax, Moroccan lamb stew and treacle sponge pudding.

Tables are simple and unadorned, bread and olives served as matter of course. Wooden wine crates stack up against pillars and keepsake bottles clutter shelves – Petrus 1978, Chateau d'Yquem 1980, Angelus 1961. "Un repas sans vin, c'est comme une equipe sans No. 10," declares a poster on the wall.

But this is still a pub in touch with its village. The

"What's important is that it's good, not where it's from, or where I'm from," says Olivier, who is proud of his varied menu. The Nepalese curry is thanks to a Nepalese cook who started out as kitchen porter and quickly impressed. Fragrant with cumin and coriander, it is the perfect vehicle for local pheasant.

Olivier gets through two whole roe deer a week in

season, and plucks and skins countless partridges, rabbits and hares. He pairs venison with winter chanterelles and ceps, picked by the kilo from secret spots. "I'd have to blindfold you if you came with me," he says, not joking.

If his butcher sees pork he considers too fatty, he saves it for Olivier: "I use all the fat in cooking somehow," he says. Occasionally he finds ox cheeks, often discarded as it costs slaughterhouses extra to cut them." Olivier braises the cheeks overnight in a neighbour's Aga, leaving two portions and a deliciously smelling house in return.

France is tapped for certain ingredients. "We buy foie gras for an occasional treat, and Dijon mustard as English doesn't cook as well. And while some British cheeses are spot on, others are over-priced. Everyone should be able

recycling and pestered the council to do more to help. Their landfill waste has now been reduced by over eighty per cent. Local mineral water was replaced by a filtering machine which also chills and carbonates, saving one hundred bottles a week. "We make less profit, but it feels better, and customers love it."

A panaché of fish – a medley of gurnard, John Dory and red mullet – and a rich fish soup sum up Olivier's approach. After filleting fish for the former, he cooks up heads and bones for a delicious fresh stock for his soup, which he flavours with home-grown fennel seeds and serves with croutons, garlic mayonnaise and grated cheese. It's absolutely delicious, whether with West Country cheddar or Gruyère.

to afford cheese." So Olivier creates Franco-English cheese plates that do not break the bank – unpasteurised Camembert, Pyrenean sheep's cheese, farmhouse cheddar and Roquefort, Stilton or Oxford Blue – whichever cheese is at its peak.

Horrified by the two-thousand-litre bin they filled each week, Olivier and Stephane introduced extensive

The Sweet Olive at The Chequers Inn

Evening main courses £12.95–£16.95
Best meal deal: lunch casserole £12.95
No food Wednesday or on Sunday evenings
Nearest train: Didcot Parkway

The White Hart

Main Road Fyfield Abingdon
Oxfordshire OX13 5LW 01865 390585
www.whitehart-fyfield.com

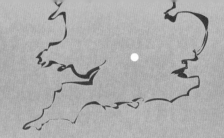

This pub's solid, white-washed and timbered exterior belies the fact that there is a jaw-dropping Great Hall, a three-storey dining room with timber arch-braced roof and minstrel's gallery. The added joy is that you get a low-ceilinged, beamed bar, too, cosy with a log fire and polished dark-wood bar.

Owner Mark Chandler is the chef, too. Entirely self-taught he never intended to end up in the kitchen when he and his wife, Kay, bought the place in 2005.

"We thought we'd both be front-of-house," says Kay, a former lawyer. "But we couldn't find a chef good enough. Meanwhile Mark was really enjoying himself in the kitchen and customers were raving about his food."

Kay and Mark were clear about what they wanted to create: "Outstanding unfussy food, affordable prices, a great atmosphere and informal service with enthusiastic staff. We rarely found that when we went out." They believe the most effective way to achieve this is to put food quality and provenance at the heart of all they do.

They have established a sizeable kitchen garden which provides most of their vegetables, fruit and herbs as well as flowers for the restaurant. A healthy bartering trade – usually for beer – with allotment-owning villagers, supplements as necessary. Meat, poultry and eggs come from local farms while fish is delivered, fresh, from Brixham market, five days a week. "Mark speaks with the suppliers the night before to see what's been landed, they barter over price, then he sits down to work out the next day's menu, " says Kay.

If the quality is right, they use organic produce and most importantly they like to know their suppliers. "Our pork comes from pigs that we know are happy and well cared for and our real ales come from small independent local breweries whose reputation depends on quality and reliability." Wines are sourced from small suppliers who have a real sense of 'terroir' and won't be found on the high street; they also stock wines from Bothy Vineyard.

Kay struggles to think of something that isn't made in the kitchens. Mark and his team conjure up bread, pasta, ice cream, petit fours, chutneys and even the horseradish sauce for roasts.

Mark's aim, says Kay, is always to let the produce shine through. "It might be complicated but it's not messed around with." You could, for example, start with home-cured salmon gravadlax with marinated cucumber salad folowed by stuffed saddle of Cotswold lamb with caper mousse, ratatouille and smoked aubergine purée. And there'll always be a balance between new and old dishes: sea bream with preserved lemon and pigs trotter compote; favourites such as fishcakes or Scotch ribeye steak with 'proper chips'.

Kay admits that at first local people were wary of them. "The previous owners had turned it into a city wine bar. We had to work hard to get the locals back on board. Once they saw that we were trying to restore the building sensitively and keeping the bar as their local, they were really supportive."

That dining room was part of a fifteenth-century priest's Chantry House and is stylishly furnished with plain wooden tables, linen napkins and black cast-iron candelabras. One of the locals always eats in the minstrel's gallery and brings firewood from his estate for the fire there in return for a bottle of claret.

They've made a real effort to be part of the community, offering free rooms for Parish Council meetings and village coffee mornings, giving talks and cooking demonstrations to local schools and establishing their car park as the village recycling point. Their staff are so enthused by Kay and Mark's approach, they even volunteer to weed the garden. "They've all got a bit of spark," says Kay. "We take them to see suppliers and, when Mark makes a new dish, everyone tries it. That way, they can give their honest recommendations."

It's hard work – just tending the garden involves a day's work a week for each of them. They could make more money by offering simpler food or taking double sittings, but Kay feels that would negate their ethos. "The atmosphere in our restaurant is about the enjoyment of food and we would hate anyone to feel rushed."

The White Hart

Evening main courses £11.50–£19
Best meal deal: set lunch 2/3 course £15/£18
No food Mondays or Sunday evening
Nearest train: Oxford

The Kingham Plough

The Green Kingham Chipping Norton
Oxfordshire OX7 6YD
01608 658327 www.thekinghamplough.co.uk

Steak and chips may sound like a standard pub dish, but here it's elevated to something special. The steak is cooked in a temperature-controlled water bath, then caramelised briefly. Chips are cooked three times, butter is spiked with grated horseradish root. Chef-proprietor Emily Watkins excels at inventive twists and her scientific approach comes from two years at the Fat Duck under Heston Blumenthal.

Having never been a head chef, let alone run a pub, taking over the Kingham Plough was bold. "I worked sixteen hours a day six days a week, running the business and covering all kitchen stations!" Her hard work paid off and the Plough, now run with husband Miles Lampson, is regularly filled. Locals call in like clockwork for drinks and homemade bar snacks of Scotch eggs, pork pies and sausage rolls. In season there are Native oysters and potted pheasant with sourdough toast (dogs get pigs' ears whatever the season).

In the restaurant the mood remains simple, with bare wooden tables and tea towel napkins, but menu descriptions belie culinary complexity. Venison might come as saddle, steamed pudding and faggot, with Jerusalem artichokes in a twice-baked soufflé, puréed and fried as crisps. 'Cotswold mess' is raspberries, cream and meringue on top of raspberry mousse and elderflower jelly, 'toffee apple' a ball of caramel-coated ice cream with a mini apple Charlotte.

Emily now employs six full-time cooks. The menu might be short, but it changes daily and there are breads, buns and biscuits to bake, sausages to stuff, bacon to cure, fish to salt, fruits to preserve and ice creams to churn. "A chain pub's staff costs would be fifteen per cent;

ours are over twice that but I'm not prepared to cut corners."

Emily and Miles are enthusiastic foragers: elderflowers are infused for gallons of cordial, and transformed into sorbets, jellies and ice creams. Plums and medlars become jams and jellies, even a membrillo-like 'cheese'. Sloes and damsons transform gin and vodka into festive treats.

Emily also hunts down old Cotswolds recipes and hams are brined, smoked and air-dried in the cellar to a late nineteenth-century Kingham Plough landlord's recipe, using the same breed of pig – the now rare 'Oxford, Sandy and Black'.

"Many pubs serve Asian stir fries made with frozen king prawns and New Zealand lamb shanks bought for less than a pound. That's not English food," asserts Emily. In place of ravioli she would urge you to try delicate dumplings stuffed with pumpkin or rabbit, and pearl barley 'risottos', enriched with bone marrow.

All produce is bought locally and green-fingered Alan Cox who has officially retired grows a profusion of tomatoes, brassicas and soft fruits for the Plough, while salad leaves come from nearby Daylesford Organic. Seafood, from mackerel to turbot, is line-caught off the South coast. And game comes courtesy of a local estate, Kingham's resident pair of rabbit-catchers and Miles.

With cheese-masters Roger Crudge and Alex James (of Blur fame) both in the village, the cheeseboard is ridiculously local. "In Italy they'd never use cheese from another region, and neither do we," says Emily, who holds farmers markets in the pub garden to help keep small suppliers like these in business.

"So many restaurants claim 'local' credentials but source from afar. At our markets customers can meet the guys who made the cheese and reared the beef and the hens who laid the eggs!"

The Kingham Plough

Evening main courses £12–£24
Shooting season game menu, 2 courses £15
Bar meals only on Sunday evening
Nearest train: Kingham

"At our markets customers can meet the guys who made the cheese and reared the beef and the hens who laid the eggs!"

The Swan at Southrop

Southrop Lechlade
Gloucestershire GL7 3NU 01367 850205
www.theswanatsouthrop.co.uk

"The fewer flavours on the plate the better. I'm not into gimmicks," says Sebastian Snow, chef proprietor at the Swan. Sebastian and wife Lana left London, where Sebastian ran four successful restaurants, to slow down in the Cotswolds. His "turf to table" approach sees local ingredients cooked simply while Lana's big personality delights all-comers.

The seventeenth-century Cotswold stone inn is part of Southrop Manor estate. Low beams, wood panelling and four open fires create the traditional backdrop and modern art adds contemporary style. In winter the skittle alley is alive with local teams and in summer it is a place for private dining under Italian chandeliers.

Sebastian's cooking career began when he was eighteen. "I had some lucky breaks and found myself in head chef positions very young, totally out of my depth. I pretended I could cook for eighteen hours a day and spent the other six buried in books trying to learn." Sebastian learnt from inspirational chefs, including Anthony Worrall Thompson, whose light touch he admired. Snows on the Green, his first London restaurant, was an instant success.

It was tempting to continue using trusted London suppliers but Sebastian set about discovering a new world of Cotswolds ingredients. "It was surprisingly easy. People offer us tons of produce and ladies from local estates come by with baskets of sorrel, nasturtiums, Swiss chard and fruit." Sebastian picks armfuls of wild garlic in spring, and strawberries, raspberries and courgette flowers in a neighbour's garden in summer. "In London those would cost a fortune," he says.

Sebastian's mother was born in Umbria and his heritage shows up in crudités with bagna cauda (a hot sauce of anchovies, garlic and butter), grilled trout with salmoriglio (an emulsion of olive oil, lemon juice, garlic and oregano), wild boar sugo on house-made pappardelle.

"As a child I spent holidays with my nonna, and would help her cooks make gnocchi; I love the authenticity and earthiness of Italian food – they don't cook to impress others. Nothing is more important than sitting down together and talking, usually about food!"

The Snows discovered that what worked in London didn't necessarily do well in the country: dishes such as slow-cooked lambs' tongues with lentils and bone marrow were hard to sell. Customers are often big meat eaters and huge game fans. So pheasant is potted for a starter; mallard fricasséed with Brussels sprouts, chestnuts and bacon; partridge roasted and served with deep-fried celeriac.

"People here are interested in provenance and hold me to account. We'll only use yellow-fin tuna and I took swordfish off the menu after a complaint. Some aren't happy about foie gras, but my roast foie gras with fried egg, toasted brioche and balsamic vinegar is a signature dish I'd be sad to lose."

A local speciality, loved by all, is wild crayfish from gravel pit lakes. "They're beautiful, chubby, tasty and cheap," enthuses Sebastian.

Autumn is his favourite season, when long evenings demand slow-cooked, warming fare. "I love using cuts not often seen in home kitchens: choucroute with ham hocks, sausages and frankfurters; belly pork with duck fat confit potatoes; pork shoulders melted down into rillettes."

Sebastian shares his knowledge at local cooking schools, and will teach at landlords Caryn and Jerry Hibbert's no-expense-spared school, Thyme at Southrop. Expect expert skills and a healthy aversion to chef trickery.

The Swan at Southrop

Evening main courses £11.25–£18
Best meal deal: 2-courses Mon-Thurs £13
No food on Sunday evenings (closed)
Nearest train: Charlbury

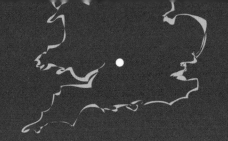

Two years living without electricity or running water in rural Kenya planted the seeds for Hilary Chester-Master's commitment to 'living lightly'. "I learnt how people can live simply yet well. There were wonderful local markets and everyone had their own vegetable garden so, however poor they were, had fantastic food." On the slopes of Mount Kenya, a world away from our horrors of waste packaging created by processed foods, virtually all food ate went full circle: seed to plate, to compost, back to seed. Another defining experience came in India where Hilary witnessed the devastating consequences of farmers switching to cash crops for export rather than for feeding the community.

Hilary was just nineteen then and had no idea that her experiences would lead her to co-run a sixteen-hundred-acre organic farm, shop and café. She and husband Will took over his family's farm near Cirencester, after his parents agreed they could turn the farm organic.

"I feel very responsible having so much land, and feel keenly it should grow food for local people. Being organic wasn't a business decision. We did it for the health of the soil, workers, wildlife and us." The farm produces beef, lamb, pork, chicken, eggs, honey, flour, fruit, vegetables, cheese, herbs, dairy products and sunflower oil. A bore hole waters the vegetables, buildings are constructed from green oak, furniture from reclaimed wood, and Gloucestershire's first woodchip boiler provides hot water and heating. There are solar panels and plans for a wind turbine to take the whole farm off-grid.

Farm shop and café are one-hundred per cent organic and, contrary to dire warnings from the business-minded, are a real success. Alongside farm produce sit a large range of organic food, ethical gifts and exquisite block-printed organic linens from Hilary's artisan workshop in Rajasthan. Cakes, ready-meals and jams are made in-house, and the squat yet flavourful loaf from Sunshine Bakery is made with Abbey flour. "Harvests were so bad

that the local mill thought our wheat was only fit for animals, but it makes our best-selling loaf!" Milk from the Shorthorns comes unhomogenised and makes cream, yogurt and cheeses, too, such as Dancy's Fancy, Ciceter Crumbly and Wiggold Cheddar.

The airy café, with garden views, veranda and wood-burner, serves rustic dishes. Meat is only served on Sundays. "I feel having anything to do with killing animals is a bad mark against my name. But I accept many people do eat meat and if it's grass-fed, and only eaten occasionally, I'm relatively comfortable with it. And it's good for the farm system." Happy cooks buzz around the kitchens and Hilary is occasionally there making preserves or chutneys from gluts of produce. To reduce dependence on electricity-guzzling freezers, Hilary's on a mission to preserve by bottling.

It took her over two years to find a cheese-maker, the assistant head grower post has remained unfilled as long, and experienced shepherds prove elusive. Realising the

skills shortage, she encouraged the Soil Association to develop an apprenticeship scheme, which she helps steer. "A lot of young people want to be growers, but most want to do their own small-scale thing. That's not going to feed the world." Abbey Home Farm and others now host two-year apprenticeships for budding farmers. "Helping kick-start that scheme is one of my main achievements."

The farm hums with activity. The Green Room hosts conferences, while the Green Kitchen offers cooking classes. Schoolchildren explore woods, meet pigs and eat their greens in the polytunnels. Visitors bump round in the trailer, and holiday-makers book yurts, cottages and campsites. Farmers come to learn from the Chester-Masters, who have won numerous awards, and queues of work experience candidates wait their turn. Hilary has more influential plans to come: a therapeutic community garden, environmental film-showings, dinners to demonstrate the diets of the world's poorest. The farm even has its own festival, Ragged Hedge Fair.

Horse & Groom

Bourton-on-the-Hill Moreton-in-Marsh
Gloucestershire GL56 9AQ
01386 700413 www.horseandgroom.info

The first forced rhubarb, multicoloured heritage tomatoes, magenta-splattered borlotti beans and the three short weeks of sweetcorn at summer's end all excite Will Greenstock, chef and joint owner of the Horse & Groom in Bourton-on-the-Hill. "I love mornings, when new produce is delivered, dictating the day's menu. It's a luxury to know I can raid the kitchen garden for more."

Will and older brother Tom bought the inn in 2005 after inhabitants of Bourton successfully kyboshed fashion tycoon George Davies's plans to convert the Georgian coaching inn, the village's only pub, into flats. When they opened, and ever since, the beautiful Cotswold stone hostelry has been filled with supportive and grateful locals and tourists.

Tom is a natural host, the young staff are chatty, the atmosphere informal. Will and Tom grew up two miles away in Blockley. Their parents Rob and Gill ran the Cotswold House Hotel in Chipping Campden, then the Howard Arms in Ilmington, both known for their food. It was perhaps inevitable that their sons' plans to study forensics and engineering faded as they discovered running a pub was much more fun.

Will worked his way up to sous chef in the Howard Arms and says: "Our parents' passion for food rubbed off on us. Before they retired we joked we were snapping at their heels and there was friendly competition. They've always been incredibly supportive, and their standard is our benchmark."

Traditional British fare is the backbone of their menu and it is infused with Mediterranean and occasional Asian flavours: roasted beetroot with fresh ricotta, tabbouleh with Swiss chard, skate with brown shrimp butter and preserved lemon, roast rump of lamb on smashed chickpeas. In summer you can eat in the garden, watch the Cotswold Legbar hens and stroll around the neat vegetable garden.

Will prefers to use whole animals from small, local farmers rather than ordering large batches of specific cuts. The menu changes during service: when the rack of lamb has gone, kebabs cut from the leg step in, later replaced, maybe, with braised shoulder. As Tom adapts the menu he shoots up and down a ladder to alter the blackboard menu. "We use all the animal so that the farmer's not left with unpopular cuts he can't sell. I get a good price, and we're forced to be creative."

Once a month Will takes a whole Dexter cow from a neighbouring farmer. After going through the steaks he makes pies, burgers and crépinettes, braises the cheeks to serve on soft polenta, uses the shins for osso bucco, and makes salt beef from the brisket to serve with horseradish crème fraiche. "The meat of this breed is sensational; the only downside is they're quite small animals, so you always want more."

The "ridiculously tasty" Tamworth is another favourite, supplied by a local farmer who researched many breeds before settling on this hardy, slow-growing ginger pig. "'Brawn' doesn't sell in the pub, but 'pork terrine' flies out!" says Will, who also makes Bath chaps and hams, puts trotters in the stock pot and sends shoulders to the butcher for sausage-making.

Seasons dictate ingredients and magazines and chefs such as Delia, Hugh and Rick give extra inspiration. "It seems obvious to say it, but things that grow together go together," says Will, who loves spring lamb with wild garlic in April, wild salmon on samphire in May, strawberry and elderflower cordial in June. The pub garden and Will's two allotments supply most produce – mustard greens, wild rocket, lambs lettuce, rainbow chard, yellow courgettes, purple sprouting broccoli – and their mother forages for wild foods.

Rich chocolate mousse with salted caramel, damson jelly with vanilla panna cotta, pear and almond tart or spiced apple flapjack crumble with thick Jersey cream from nearby Holmleigh farm make it hard to pass on the puddings. "Coffee is from Gloucester-based Ethical Addictions who tour coffee growers around the world and set up better-than

fairtrade deals." Fair trade, of course, is a cornerstone of the Slow Food movement.

"An important aspect of 'Slow Food' is also that it should be produced at nature's speed and eaten in season," says Tom. "We shouldn't expect to have what we want when we want it. That means, for example, no tomatoes for most of the year. You can try asking Will for one in December, but you won't get far. It's worth the wait. We get really excited when they return!"

Horse & Groom

Evening main courses £10–£18
Most dishes can be adapted for children
No food on Sunday evening
Nearest train: Moreton-in-Marsh

Fancy a night with the pigs? This is not reality television, but Helen Browning's ploy for enticing people onto her farm in the Wiltshire Downs. Guests camp with the Saddlebacks then head to Helen's pub, the Royal Oak, for 'Pigstock', the village of Bishopstone's very own rock and pork festival.

"It's all about having fun, watching the animals and learning by seeing for yourself," says Helen, who prefers to engage people rather than lecture to them about the high animal welfare standards her mixed farm exemplifies. Having developed a name nationally via supermarket sales of her exceptional bacon and sausages and her national delivery service, Helen decided it was time she met her customers, and they met the animals.

Helen was just twenty-four when her father handed her the reins of Eastbrook Farm, near Swindon. Having seen the detrimental effect on wildlife of hedges being ripped out to create vast fields, and been sickened by the intensive pig and poultry farming methods she witnessed at agricultural college, Helen decided to run her farm organically. Young and female, agrichemical salesmen assumed she'd be a soft target, but all were sent packing up the farm track.

Starting with two British Saddlebacks in 1987, Helen pioneered the organic system for rearing pigs on a large scale. The three-thousand piglets born each year suckle for two months, then range free on clover-rich pastures in family groups. Sows are not imprisoned in farrowing crates, and no pig is castrated, has its teeth cut or tail docked. Like cattle, sheep and chickens, her pigs are rotated for grazing to outwit species-specific parasites.

It may surprise some that Helen, who puts animal welfare at the top of her agenda, produces veal "for animal welfare reasons". It's hard to argue with her reason: "Female calves are kept as dairy stock but the males, which do not usually make good beef cattle,

are often shot at birth and I couldn't bear to do that. It seemed such a waste. I let them suckle on foster mums and live normal, natural lives for eight months."

Calves are suckled rather than fed powdered formula, which Helen believes improves animal health and meat quality. "The foster mum's tender loving care makes a difference, too. They show the calves how to find shade and water and keep them happy and relaxed."

Helen chairs the Food Ethics Council and was instrumental in leading the growth of the Soil Association. She received an OBE for services to organic farming. "Some feel threatened by organic farming as it criticises the norm, and organic farmers don't buy as much. We don't fit into the usual economic framework."

Fed up with having nowhere exceptional to eat out, Helen and partner Tim Finney took over the Royal Oak, Helen's favourite pub since her teenage years. "We wanted to develop a local food community; it's an elbows on the table, dog underneath kind of place, with a great gang of regular drinkers."

Chef Liz Franklin has the pleasure of cooking meat from Eastbrook and nearby Laverstoke Park, fish fresh off the Lady Hamilton day-boat from Newlyn, vegetables from Coleshill walled garden, garden fruit and herbs, and whatever she forages on the way to work – nettles for soup in spring, sloes for gin in autumn. Villagers grow

heirloom tomatoes and salad leaves in return for dinner or pints of Arkells real ale.

Some of Helen's pork travels overseas. "The British are big bacon-eaters and the continentals are bigger ham-eaters so we export surplus pork leg and as a nation import bacon. Other cuts go to Germany, home of the sausage, and they make the most amazing preservative-free salami for us."

So are the extra food miles justified in such cases? "We've traded for thousands of years and it would be hard to go from flying in most things to nothing. Sensible trade can help people form connections and be less parochial."

Ponder that as you follow in the footsteps of Stone Age man on Britain's oldest road, the chalk Ridgeway. Collect a picnic from the pub, or time your return for one of the DIY barbecues in the garden. If lucky, you'll be handed some excess eggs from the resident chickens when you leave. If not, buy them in the shop. Then join a summer evening tour to meet the animals.

"I'm excited about how consumers are engaging with food and farming and taking their future into their own hands. There is a great awareness of Community Supported Agriculture and school-farm partnerships and so many are signing up for beekeeping, cheese-making and horticulture classes. Perhaps the bubble of endless consumerism and capitalism at all costs has been pricked?"

The Potting Shed Pub

Crudwell Malmesbury
Wiltshire SN16 9EW 01666 577833
www.thepottinghshedpub.com

When Jonathan and Julian, at twenty-five and thirty-five years old, arrived in Crudwell from London and bought the Rectory Hotel, then the pub opposite, villagers feared the worst and predicted swanky dining and lack of space for those who were there for a drink rather than dinner. Changing the pub's name from The Plough to The Potting Shed was the last straw. "It stirred up a hornets' nest. But our intention was only to create a successful village pub. Winning an award as the UK's best new pub convinced us we had done the right thing."

After a string of reviews and awards, and an investment in community relations, all was forgiven. Sponsorship of the football team, open doors for school visits, hog roasts at village events, barbecues, support for the fête – all helped the Potting Shed to become part of village life. When Jonathan and Julian extended their vegetable plot and offered ten raised beds to villagers the response was overwhelming.

"It's been fantastic getting to know everyone. People come in muddy-booted from the garden, aching for a pint. Or bring friends to admire their vegetables then have lunch. We're offered their gluts, and weave them into the menu. Back in London we didn't know our neighbours, let alone share food. Here we even know their dogs and have jars of biscuits for them on the bar."

Jonathan and Julian subscribe to Slow Food values. On arriving in the Cotswolds, they scoured farmers' markets for the best (often organic) suppliers. "It's about reflecting local flavours, supporting good businesses and finding the tastiest ingredients. We shouldn't be flying in whatever whenever just because we can." 'Tipples of the day' are bubbly cocktails flavoured with Esther Chapman's Cotswold

liqueurs: elderflower, raspberry, blackberry, damson, quince and sloe made just the other side of Stroud. Meat is sourced from a Cirencester butcher, game from nearby farmers and vegetables from well-grilled suppliers. "Our chefs quiz delivery men to check it's the local, organic produce we ordered. If we discovered we were being given something else we'd switch supplier," says Jonathan.

Dreams to grow their own vegetables faded as realities emerged. So beds of carrots, beans and potatoes, of which they could never grow enough, were replaced with mixed leaves, herbs, broad beans, baby beetroot and radishes. A fruit cage is next, if cooks can agree what to plant. "Growing your own isn't cheaper but it gives us great pleasure. I never knew chefs could be so passionate about salad!"

Young chef Dan Wyatt, who trained over at the Rectory, has a passion for careful sourcing that won him the job. When the menu changes each month, he researches old British classics, then adds his own update: lamb, rosemary and redcurrant burger with tomato jam and mint mayonnaise; lardy cake with English breakfast

tea ice cream; rhubarb and pistachio Eton mess.

"Dan makes everything except the bread himself," says Jonathan "and his ice creams – Turkish Delight, Baileys, cinnamon and calvados – are phenomenal. He loves making pasta and giving the sauce or stuffing a local flavour, such as wild rabbit or pheasant. In fact, for him, the more labour-intensive the better; he'd be making rook pie if we could source enough!"

Menus, particularly at lunch, include triple-cooked chip butties with house-made ketchup, lamb casserole with pearl barley in its own cast iron pot, Gloucester Old Spot sausages with mash, spiced rice pudding with plum jam. River Exe mussels in a creamy cider and bacon sauce had diners driving from Bristol, and Sunday roasts draw a hundred. Sunday evenings see a mellow crowd nibbling leftover roast potatoes and crackling at the bar and taking up the fortnightly offer of a quiz with a pint of real ale and scoop of communal pie.

Even the smart if quirky makeover has won its place in people's affections. "We wanted to reflect our personal style and passions," says Jonathan, who had grown disillusioned with his previous job in an increasingly corporate hotel chain.

Julian's background in art- and antique-dealing accounts for fitting eccentricities: wheelbarrow light shades, garden fork handled beer pumps, sacking on cushions, butcher's block tables.

"We love the pub," says Jonathan, "and although we've both been hugely interested in food all our lives, thanks to our mothers, we wanted this to be as much a drinking pub as dining destination."

The Potting Shed Pub

Evening main courses £11–£18
Barbecues, spit roasts and wine dinners organised
No food Sunday evening
Nearest train: Kemble

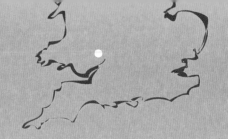

The Mill Race
Walford Ross-on-Wye
Herefordshire HR9 5QS
01989 562891 www.millrace.info

In 2004, when Luke Freeman bought The Mill Race near Ross-on-Wye, it was a dingy and run-down pub. Now, with cherry red walls, a granite bar, a wood-burning stove, local artwork and a book-swap corner it's smart yet homely and, over the intervening years, has become central to community life here in the Wye Valley.

The pub likes to involve villagers in activities such as cooking demonstrations and runs a popular children's menu competition. "Children are asked to put together a healthy balanced menu, using local produce," says Hayley Coombs, their marketing person. "The winner's menu is used in the pub for twelve months."

An annual 'Food Fair' forges further links with the community and there are proposals to build a new farm shop as an extension of the pub. "Lots of customers have said they would like somewhere to buy the ingredients we use," says Hayley. "We already sell hampers of local produce and the shop seems like a natural progression which will give the village a much-needed amenity."

The Mill Race's menu offers pub classics and bistro-style dishes, or you can opt for a 'takeaway'. The latter, Hayley explains: "A few people came in for drinks and asked to take something home to eat. We plated up a few meals and the next day the plates came back. It went down well so we decided to do it properly; our fish and chips is undoubtedly a favourite."

The pub's surroundings make food sourcing a joy. "We're in a fabulous position, surrounded by high quality farmland," says Hayley. "Cobrey Farm, one of the UK's biggest asparagus growers, is two miles from us; E C Drummond & Son, a soft fruit grower is three miles away; a local smallholding supplies us with rare breed Tamworth pigs and all their fresh flowers and people regularly drop by with produce for us to try."

Owner Luke's family also owns a one-thousand-acre farm, with shoot and woodland, two miles from the pub, that supplies them with beef, game, wild rabbits, poultry and wild boar as well as all the wood for the logburner; staff and chefs forage for wild garlic, mushrooms and berries and local villagers bring in gluts of plums and apples from their gardens.

Up to ninety per cent of their ingredients (fish aside) come from within twenty miles; ales and ciders are locally brewed. Local abundance doesn't guarantee quality, though. "So," says Hayley, "our chefs visit new suppliers and constantly monitor things."

Popular dishes include ham, egg and chips, smoked haddock risotto, and roast hake with cockle and chive butter, field mushrooms and garlic tagliatelle. Staff taste each and know how it's made; all undergo wine training; and everyone is encouraged to come up with ideas. "Sourcing fish can be more tricky and we try to only use UK indigenous species and follow Marine Conservation Society guidelines. Our sous chef is a keen fisherman and regularly catches trout and salmon for the kitchen."

A chalk board, with a map of Herefordshire and surrounding counties, details their suppliers and the food miles of menu items. Everything is made onsite except bread and ice cream. Says Hayley: "Rowlestone Farm's ice cream is unbeatable: the farm began making it to increase the income from their dairy herd so we're delighted to support that."

"The Mill Race's menu offers pub classics and bistro-style dishes, or you can opt for a 'takeaway'"

September Organic

Whitehill Park Weobley
Herefordshire HR4 8QE 01544 312910
www.september-organic.co.uk

"The best ice cream is made to a simple recipe with pure ingredients." Adam Glyn-Jones' mission is straightforward: to make delicious ice cream using the best cream, milk and eggs, and not much else. "We want to make something you could create in your own kitchen," explains Adam, who therefore leaves out artificial emulsifiers, stabilisers, colours or flavours.

The Glyn-Jones family started making ice cream in 1987 when quotas limited the milk they could sell. For the first seventeen years milk, cream and eggs all came from the family farm in Herefordshire. But in May 2003 they received their first positive bovine Tuberculosis test results, and within six weeks almost all their cows were slaughtered. "We'd spent twenty-five years building up our pedigree herd," says Adam. "The prefix for the herd was 'September' and then we named each cow after a species of bird. We'd known whole families, from great grandmothers to great granddaughters. Losing the herd was a huge emotional wrench and we didn't have the heart or energy to resume dairy farming."

Over twenty-five thousand cattle are slaughtered annually in the UK due to bovine TB. "The connection to badgers is irrefutable," says Adam, "but so far little has been done about them. Culling may only be part of the solution though. Stressed cows are more susceptible to disease, and both badgers and cattle often have a selenium deficiency, which increases their chance of contracting TB. So that needs to be addressed."

The compensation that Adam's parents received was put into the ice cream business that they handed over to Adam and his wife Liz. His parents now pour their energy into CountrySOLE, their sustainable living project based around two 'eco-cabins' and a circular garden grown on permaculture principles where guests can harvest

their own veg. "Protecting the environment is the core of our philosophy," says Adam. His parents were influenced in the sixties by Rachel Carson's 'Silent Spring', a book that portrays an eerily quiet countryside where pesticides have eradicated the birds.

A herd of Jerseys eight miles away provides the rich milk for the September range and cream comes from Gloucestershire. Adam's sister Bridie Whittle runs The Good Egg Company on the family farm, so her small flocks of hens provide the eggs.

Customers love their classic British flavours, including elderflower, blackberry and apple crumble, strawberry, lemon tea and Christmas pudding. Adam's favourite is brown bread, the first they made. New suggestions come from customers and staff, and Adam is working with a local fruit farm to increase the number of ingredients he can source locally. "Few farmers are interested in selling manufacturing grade fruit, so if it's less than perfect it's often left to rot in the field."

People used to freeze their 'cream ices' by standing pots in buckets of ice and salt; the salt lowers the freezing

point of the melting ice, something understood as early as the thirteenth century in the Arab world and later relayed to Italy and France. To create a smoother texture, cooks learnt to hand-churn the mixture as it froze. Now Adam uses modern technology to combine sugars and fats to produce 3,600 litres a week. "Making ice cream is not great as far as energy efficiency is concerned," admits Adam, "but the hot water generated from refrigeration is used in sinks and for cleaning, and a specially designed tower recycles and naturally cools water for cooling machinery. There is little 'green' equipment available for a medium-sized dairy like ours so we've had to devise our own low-tech solutions."

Adam and Liz worked for Voluntary Service Overseas encouraging farmers to diversify from water-intensive rice production into dairy farming and therefore satisfying domestic demand for milk in Westernised cities. Their work inspired them to create a fairtrade range: "Having worked in the developing world, we know the impact low prices can have on a family and community."

September Organic ice cream is up to fourteen times the price of the cheapest supermarket incarnation. "You cannot compare the two," says Adam, "our product is just unfortunate to share the name. To be 'ice cream', a product needs only to contain at least two and a half per cent fat – and that's any fat – and at least two per cent milk solids. That's it." Adam's vanilla contains one quarter pure cream and all his ice creams contain milk, cream and eggs – surprisingly elusive in most ice creams. "Ice cream should be a treat, an occasional indulgence. In that remit ours is healthy as we use all natural ingredients. It's psychologically good for you too!"

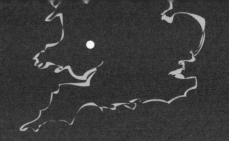

Dunkertons
Pembridge Leominster
Herefordshire HR6 9ED
01544 388653 www.dunkertons.co.uk

When Ivor and Susie Dunkerton started making organic cider and perry at their farm in Herefordshire in the eighties, farm production had all but disappeared as industrially–produced brands dominated the market. Many orchards were scrubbed up, and fruit that remained was sold to factory producers or left to rot in the grass.

"We needed to make our smallholding viable, so settled on cider and haven't looked back," says Ivor, who first came to Herefordshire on honeymoon and fell in love with its rolling hills, orchards and wild flowers.

The farm's previous owner, a teetotaller, had ripped out the cider apple orchard so Ivor and Susie planted anew and have been steadily and successfully expanding

producer. As Dunkertons expands, more local orchards are going into organic production.

Following the Conquest, Norman cider-making techniques spread to southern England. Pressing hedgerow crab apples to release their alcoholic potential was probably common but by the seventeenth century it had become an art form, with Herefordshire leading the way; cider and perry were treated like fine wines by Georgian London's elite and sipped like champagne.

When over a century of wars between England and France came to an end in the early eighteen hundreds, French wine flooded back to English cellars, and cider and perry were shunned. Later the Truck Acts forbade alcohol to be paid in lieu of farm workers' wages, which

and annexing orchards on local farms ever since.

"When we arrived there were yellowhammers, curlews, hares, hedgehogs and foxes, and we'd often hear owls shrieking during the day. But they've pretty much disappeared, which I put down to the sprays used in farming," says Ivor, who's held organic certification for his cider and perry longer than any other Herefordshire

significantly dented farmhouse cider-making. The twentieth century saw the rise of several commercial brands – who could forget the Babycham years – and an image problem for two of England's oldest drafts.

"People thought of cider as cheap and nasty, and associated it with drunken teenagers. We wanted to bring it upmarket by creating a better flavoured product

through traditional methods, to be drunk like wine. The large manufacturers produce an industrialised product but their hefty advertising has re-popularised cider. We don't spend a penny on publicity yet struggle to keep up with demand," says Ivor.

From October to December, the Dunkertons' farm is awash with the aromas of freshly crushed pears and apples. After milling, pulp is pressed to extract juice, surprisingly sweet given the inedibility of the fruit, which then ferments all winter until natural sugars are used up. The cider is then stored in two giant oak vats that are named Adam and Eve.

Sulphur dioxide is added to prevent spoilage but even less is added than the small amount allowed by the Soil

perfumed, and White Norman adds tannic structure," explains Ivor, who relies on Susie's exceptional palate to get the balance right. The blends vary each year, but are created from a palette of thirty varieties.

To celebrate twenty-eight years of production – "why wait for thirty?" – the Dunkertons have produced a special vintage cider – strong, rich, fruity and slightly sweet. There are also sparkling and still blends ranging from dry to medium sweet – excellent with curry – and single variety ciders too. Black Fox – named after a dark beast lurking in the orchards fleetingly glimpsed by Susie – is robust, peaty and perfect with mature cheddar.

Elegant and ambrosial, their sparkling perry makes a sophisticated aperitif. Perry is pressed from Moorcroft

Association. Organic sugar is used to sweeten dry cider to medium cider, and water is only added if the alcohol content rises too high.

The art of cider-making lies in blending the separately fermented juices. "We use a mild variety – like Sheep's Nose, one of the oldest, or Sweet Coppin – then add other dimensions. Foxwhelp is very acidic and the most highly

pears, also known as Stinking Bishop, which gave its name to the odoriferous Gloucestershire cheese washed in perry as it matures. Moorcrofts can rot from within, so Ivor has planted twelve other varieties including Red Horse, Gin, Merrylegs and Judge Amphlett; many pears have made it off the endangered list thanks to the growing band of perry makers and support from the Slow Food movement.

Upper Wick Farm

Rushwick
Worcestershire WR2 5SU
01905 422243 www.rootsatrushwick.co.uk

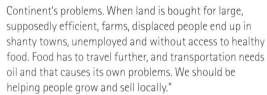

Will Edmonds and wife Meg returned to his family's farm in Rushwick, near Worcester, with a mission to grow organic food for a local market. Starting with beef, lamb and cereals for feed, the enterprise grew to include chicken, eggs, fruit, vegetables, herbs, apple juice and honey as villagers pestered them for more. "We had eighty neighbours peering over the fence, intrigued to see what else we could grow."

Kingfishers, woodpeckers, buzzards and owls also make Upper Wick Farm their home, which is partially framed by the beautiful river Teme that snakes around the southwest border. It regularly bursts its banks, bringing clean water, nutrients and seeds to the ancient grasslands, thus providing a rich, natural diet for Will's cows and sheep.

Continent's problems. When land is bought for large, supposedly efficient, farms, displaced people end up in shanty towns, unemployed and without access to healthy food. Food has to travel further, and transportation needs oil and that causes its own problems. We should be helping people grow and sell locally."

Will practises what he preaches: produce is sold through Roots at Rushwick farmshop, and through a second shop near Ledbury and never to distant retailers. Food-lovers at the Cheltenham and Ludlow farmers' markets make a beeline for their homegrown produce, including pak choi and borlotti beans.

In the shops, produce from twenty other local farmers finds shelf space, alongside jams, pickles and cheeses.

Will had grown disillusioned with his previous job selling animal feed and chemical sprays. "There was a move towards Genetically Modified strains and, while I feel scientific advances play a role in agriculture, I hate GM being pushed on people by big business."

The worldwide trend for merging small farms into bigger units employing fewer people concerns Will deeply. "This is happening in Africa and it is not the answer to the

Particularly popular are Hereford Hop, which evolved from the practice of preserving cheese in barrels of hops, and Saint Eadburgha, a Camembert-like cheese from Broadway in the Cotswolds.

To meet customer demand, especially in winter, produce is sometimes imported.

"International trade can be good, especially for developing nations," says Will, "but if you want a vibrant countryside and fresh food, you should buy British."

Having something for everyone, at affordable prices, is crucial say Will and Meg. "We'll sell half a courgette and two eggs to an elderly lady living on her own, and huge sacks of potatoes at twenty pence a kilo to families on tight budgets." Their organic, grass-fed beef and lamb is comparable in price to that in a conventional butchers, and cheaper than in some supermarkets.

Black Rock hens wander freely in the ancient cherry orchard and eggs are sold still warm from the nest. "Truly fresh eggs hold their shape when poached, and sit right up in the frying pan."

Table birds live for a minimum of ninety days rather than the usual forty, and are killed, hung and dry-plucked

it themselves means the Edmonds employ more workers than is usual for a farm this size. "Everyone does everything, so the person selling you your courgette knows why we grow yellow ones (they hold their shape better when cooking) and may have picked it themselves that morning." And Meg finds nothing gets a team meeting off to a better start than convening around a table filled with home-cooked dishes.

Meg spearheaded Marks & Spencer's 'Select Farm' food scheme and loves her hands-on role. She grows fruit, flowers, herbs and salads, and bakes cakes for the café.

Through Upper Wick's 'Food for Life' partnership with Four Dwellings School in Birmingham, pupils see organic farming in action and glean tips for their school

onsite. "People don't realise supermarkets sell such young birds. Ours have proper skeletal structures and proportioned bodies, with more defined and flavoured leg meat, and we hand-pluck them giving skin that crisps beautifully." Will cannot bring himself to describe the wet-plucking process of industrial chicken processing, it is too disgusting.

Growing a variety of foods and processing and selling

allotment. "We hammer home the connections between hens, eggs, slaughter room and meat; you can see realisation dawning!" Some already understand, especially, Will notes, those from Africa and Asia.

Public open days feature bee-keeping and vegetable-growing workshops. "We feel privileged to live here. It's a way of life vanishing fast. Our children are getting a taste of it, and we want to share it with others too."

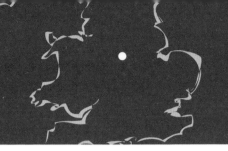

Manor Farm

77 Main Street Long Whatton Loughborough
Leicestershire LE12 5DF 01509 646413
www.manororganicfarm.co.uk

Vivienne Matravers has wanted to be a farmer since she was four. "I used to travel with my mother recording wildflowers for a wildlife trust. As soon as my parents let me, I helped out on greenbelt farms. Later, as an agricultural advisor, I learned the extent to which chemical sprays were used and it made it obvious how many flowers were under threat."

Vivienne and her husband Graeme took on Manor Farm, part of the Paget estate, with a desire to make it an organic enterprise specialising in beef, lamb and poultry. Now their land is festooned with the blooms of Vivienne's childhood: pink campion, lady's smock, figwort, celandines, speedwells.

Manor Farm's three-hundred organic acres of softly undulating Leicestershire countryside is mostly clover-rich pasture for the entirely grass-fed Longhorn Cross beef cattle and pedigree Lleyn sheep. Table chickens are reared free-range during the summer and turkeys are introduced in July to grow slowly in time for Christmas.

Government grants and the estate helped the Matravers restore the listed cow byres that now house the shop, bakery and butchery. Built around a courtyard in a style traditional to the region, each building has been renovated reusing valuable local stone and slate.

The shops are open Wednesday to Saturday and are 'real' farm shops, says Vivienne. "We sell the genuine article, not like those pseudo shops that aren't run by farmers. We want people to associate the food they cook for their family with the farm that produced it. Everything is organic except the honey, and we source as locally as possible." Pork is from neighbours Richard and Inger Mee, milk and cream from Lubcloud Farm, also on the Paget Estate, eggs from Sutton Bonington, and fruit and vegetables from Lincolnshire, which is about as far as Vivienne's prepared to go to source fresh produce.

There's locally milled flour too, some from their own wheat.

"Opening the shop was in keeping with organic farming's holistic approach. Our philosophy is to sell locally and spend locally." The Manor Farm shop provides a community resource and a hub that's akin to the general store and post offices so sadly missing from rural villages. Vivienne reckons ninety per cent of customers come from within fifteen miles, and most return week in week out, appreciating the friendly banter. All are welcome to walk around the farm trail, too.

"Organic food has a reputation for being expensive, but our beef and lamb prices are brilliant. With mince for example, the difference is pence not pounds. With poultry and pork there is a bigger jump between conventional and organic because of how the animals are reared."

Slaughtering is a big issue and the animals travel several junctions down the M1 to Joseph Morris, one of the first organically registered abattoirs in the country. "It's great, but further away than we'd like," admits Vivienne, who laments the shortage of abattoirs available for small producers. Chickens are sent for dispatch just down the road at biodynamic Hungary Lane Farm, which also supplies the shop with chicken when home-reared birds run out.

Manor Farm employs six people, far more than other three-hundred-acre farms, supporting research that organic farms provide thirty-two per cent more jobs than conventional equivalents. Karl Hughes, a baker since he was fifteen, enthusiastically knocks up organic breads, tarts and other treats. "He skilfully blends our flour with stronger flours to get the right rise," says Vivienne, who loves his spelt bread and crusty Coburg domes. Karl runs occasional classes so visitors can learn tricks of the trade. The vastly-experienced butcher, Martin Bilson, makes sausages, burgers and bacon; his Sicilian-style sausages are especially popular.

Each year hundreds of schoolchildren, scouts, gardeners and other farmers visit Manor Farm to tour the land, join an event or admire the native Longhorns that are far gentler than their looks suggest. They are told how the rich birdlife – buzzards, woodpeckers, owls, yellowhammers and swallows – indicate the vibrant insect population and how that population is due to the grazing animals and banks of wild flowers. Children go pond-dipping and coo over newborn lambs. "Their visits can be life-changing for them and spending time with youngsters is one of the most important parts of what we do."

"Opening the shop was in keeping with organic farming's holistic approach. Our philosophy is to sell locally and spend locally"

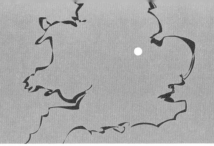

"The Olive Branch is more than a pub, it's a community project, too," says Ben Jones who, with old friends Sean Hope and Marcus Welford, managed to get their hands on the pub before it was sold as a house. Locals were delighted: with no local shop or post office, the Olive Branch was vital.

Having worked in smart restaurants, hotels and wineries, the trio happily returned to their home county excited about doing their own thing simply with the region's best ingredients. They thought they'd left behind the world of the Michelin star but one day a friend called and told them to look in the new Michelin guide. "We had no idea we were even being considered," recalls Ben, "but

Sean launched his restaurant career right here – as a teenager washing pots. He now creates British classics: pea and ham soup with crispy bacon, char-grilled ribeye steak with homemade chips, Lincolnshire sausages with mustard mash and red cabbage, sticky toffee pudding. Best-selling fish and chips come as crispy goujons of pollack, whiting or coley (in place of less sustainable cod or haddock) with minted peas and tomato fondue.

A perfect pork and stilton pie is made locally to Sean's recipe and served with nutty Sparkenhoe Red Leicester made with a local farm's unpasteurised cow's milk and house-made piccalilli and chutney. Other favourite dishes are artichoke and wild garlic risotto, brill with scallop

there we were!" Only one other pub had ever been awarded a star before theirs, so its impact was significant and the business soon expanded to include a second pub, the Red Lion in Stathern, and later the Beech House, a luxury B&B opposite the Olive Branch.

Inside the beautiful stone house you can see the frame of the three cottages that were knocked together - now they are cosy interconnected dining areas. Low beams, old wooden furniture, open fires, the chatter of happy diners and genuinely enthusiastic staff put people at ease. "We like to generate rapport with our customers, so we can tell them about our food and encourage them to try new things," explains Ben.

ravioli and shellfish bisque and Chantenay carrot cake with pistachio ice cream. Presentation is elegant, not fussy; this is gastropub food at its best.

Sean loves nothing more than driving around Rutland, Leicestershire and Lincolnshire meeting his producers and discovering new ones, chatting to farmers, tasting and plotting the next local ingredient to bring to the menu. When he was working in large city restaurants, producers were distant voices at the end of the telephone. Now, knowing them personally brings many rewards.

For example, when Sean couldn't get his favourite bread anymore - a traditional Rearsby loaf made with honey and pumpkin seeds - he worked with Mick Smith at

mushroom forager Clive Holder, Rainbow, a local food co-operative and J D Papworth traditional butchers and graziers are some of Strattons' suppliers and Vanessa plans a farmers' market in the garden and a deli-cum-coffee shop to showcase them and others.

Chef Simon Linacre-Marshall applies his classical French training to ingredients for which the Brecks, the central area of Norfolk, is renowned: griddled asparagus with hollandaise, wild mushroom risotto with beetroot carpaccio and truffle, rabbit and partridge terrine with damson jelly, venison with sour cherry sauce, lavender ice cream with honey and blueberry cheesecake. He enjoys the challenge of keeping it local, seasonal and to a large extent organic, knowing that Vanessa and Les will not tolerate rogue ingredients.

Brian Wilson from Beachamwell and a local network of growers supply vegetables; figs, white peaches, grapes, quinces and plums ripen here on south-facing walls.

"We demonstrate that eating British vegetables all year need not be boring. Simon makes a cauliflower crème caramel spiked with chilli as a starter, which is absolutely delicious, and a wonderful butternut squash and goat's cheese gratin. You can create surprising and incredible

results from the most simple ingredients," says Vanessa.

Hens roam the Scotts' orchard, nibbling scraps, fertilising soil and yielding orange-yolked eggs. The use of raw yolks in mayonnaise prompted a battle with environmental health officers, a story Vanessa relates to highlight disconnection with food production. "Our freshly laid eggs are much healthier than those from factory farms, which sit around for weeks. Eggs – a human food for millennia – are treated like lethal weapons, while people guzzle Coca-Cola!"

Vanessa finds cooks straight from catering college clueless about seasonality, organic farming, recycling and conserving energy, so retrains them herself. She encourages guests to slow down, too, and connect with the Brecks. "Just taking a walk in the countryside connects them to the natural world not noticed from fast cars."

Strattons

Evening main courses £16–£26
Best meal deal: Lunch, £9
Food always available
Nearest train: Downham Market

The White Horse

Brancaster Staithe
Norfolk PE31 8BY 01485 210262
www.whitehorsebrancaster.co.uk

Cliff Nye grew up with the fishermen of the north Norfolk coast, holidaying in Brancaster Staithe and learning to sail from its harbour. He loved it so much that after making his money manufacturing windows he returned to buy a house, then a pub, and then another pub with a brewery attached. "The White Horse had become very rundown, with a tatty caravan park out the back and a kitchen full of microwaves. If I hadn't saved it, it would've ultimately closed down."

Cliff added a handsome conservatory dining room, sun deck and several bedrooms that are sunk into the land that slopes down to the sea. Wife Tina's contemporary style – all natural materials and seascape colours – blends in perfectly. The view could not be more 'Norfolk': past the coastal footpath at the bottom of the garden stretches a labyrinth of marshes and waterways dotted with brightly painted moored dinghies, with Scolt Head Island's dunes and the sea beyond. Tens of thousands of Arctic pink-

footed geese winter here, their silhouettes and calls fill the sky each evening.

Cliff's old fishermen pals, now accompanied by the children and grandchildren who followed them to sea, are regulars "and not shy about telling me how they'd like their pub run!" Ales are brewed by son James from local ingredients: hoppy Oystercatcher, bottle conditioned Brancaster Best, Malthouse Bitter and SS Viner. Cliff and Tina's friendly staff, an informal atmosphere and skilful modern British cooking draw local stalwarts, families on holiday and weekenders.

Mussels and oysters are staples, at their best in winter when fat and meaty rather than milky from summer spawning. Cyril Southerland – "an authority on the water" – and son Ben work from a shed within diners' view, bagging mussels picked by hand from carefully tended short stretches of tidal creeks called 'lays'. They harvest young mussels from offshore sandbanks during the summer months, then let them grow in lays closer by; simply steamed open with white wine, cream and parsley, they are plump, sweet and delicious.

Rock oysters travel metres not miles, too. Cultivated from 'seed' in the harbour by Richard Loose, they are served raw or tempura-battered and fried so fast they are still slippery fresh inside their hot, crispy exterior. Cockles, another ancient Norfolk coast speciality, appear when fat, hand-harvested specimens are found. "With shellfish you have to know exactly where and when it was collected. Knowing fishermen in Norfolk as we do gives us complete confidence. That's a privilege and you can absolutely taste the freshness," says Cliff.

Crab and lobster are caught locally in pots by Simon Letzer and come either simply dressed or in hand-made ravioli with brandied shellfish cream. "Our suppliers know us and they're honest about their catch. Simon will steer us away from the temptingly beautiful lobster to the one covered in scars and barnacles. The unscathed specimen will have shed its shell recently and be pumped full of water to stretch out its new skin, whereas the other will be meatier."

Simon's father Paul runs a smokehouse four miles away and brings salmon, kippers and undyed smoked haddock for White Horse breakfasts. "Their kippers are

smoked naturally over oak and are simply the best."

A daily specials menu offers local day-boat catches: sea bass, mackerel, lemon sole, sea trout and mullet. Cliff is not alone among the restaurateurs in this book as he tussles with the customers' desire for unsustainable fish such as halibut, cod, monkfish and salmon.

Cliff sources these fish from wholesalers and says, "We try to go for more sustainable options, but our reality is marketplace prices and customer demand, so it's not always possible."

Norfolk beef, lamb, pork, pheasant, partridge, venison and wildfowl are on the menu, too. Fruit and vegetables are mostly seasonal and include Norfolk asparagus in spring, marsh samphire and fat blueberries in late summer and curly kale and apples in autumn. The cheeseboard showcases the county's finest varieties, such as Mrs Temple's soft Wighton, matured Walsingham and creamy Binham Blue, all made in small quantities

from the milk of her own herd near Wells-next-the-Sea.

The incredibly hard-working and energetic chef, Rene Llupar, has learnt to do things 'The White Horse way' and he finds the extra time needed to work with individual fishermen. As Cliff says, "there are benefits other than commercial ones to keeping it local. These fishermen were my main motivation for buying the pub. They're the centre of the community, and they're my oldest friends."

The White Horse

Evening main courses £10.95–£16.95
Breakfast and bar menus available all day
Daily and monthly changing menus
Nearest train: Kings Lynn

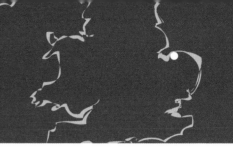

Courtyard Farm
Ringstead Hunstanton
Norfolk PE36 5LQ
01485 525251 www.courtyardfarm.co.uk

Lord Peter Melchett has never tasted the pork and beef that he rears at Courtyard Farm and sells in local farm shops. "My children tell me it's very good," he says. Peter stopped eating meat in the seventies for philosophical reasons. But when he converted to organic farming – primarily to save wildlife being destroyed by intensive practices – he needed animals.

"We need mixed, organic farming, which uses livestock, to combat climate change and other threats to wildlife and food security," says Peter. "We must eat less meat: factory farmed pork and poultry is unsustainable, and cruelly manipulates animals like cogs in an industrial machine. But grass-fed red meat is good for us, for animals and for the planet. Emissions from cattle and

sheep grazing on well-managed pasture are balanced by carbon which the grassland stores."

Conker-coloured Red Poll cattle, a traditional East Anglian breed, graze on species-rich grassland and freshwater marshes. Their leafy diet keeps them healthy and results in meat higher in beneficial Omega-3 fatty acids, Beta-carotene and vitamins A and E than that from grain-fed cattle. "A climate-friendly diet is also a healthy diet," says Peter.

Saddleback and Tamworth sows are crossed with Duroc boars to produce delicious porkers. Unlike their intensively farmed cousins, who exist in cramped conditions on concrete floors, the pigs at Courtyard Farm live in family groups and enjoy space to range. If all pork

was produced this way there would be less on sale and it would be expensive but the extra-tasty meat would be a treat worth waiting for.

"Converting a large arable farm to organic requires introducing animals, more workers and new rotation systems and machinery. Few will risk the outlay." But Peter believes change is inevitable: artificial fertilisers are unsustainable since their manufacture relies on fossil fuels and dwindling supplies of mined phosphorus. Courtyard Farm still produces grain, but now legumes and livestock provide natural fertility.

Peter has been a university lecturer, Labour government minister and leader of several conservation NGOs. He is now the Soil Association's policy director. His father bought Courtyard Farm, formerly part of Hunstanton Estate, in 1959, and Peter grew up nearby.

"I remember the sky filled with wave after wave of lapwings, and fields of stubble erupting with starlings, corn buntings, tree sparrows and skylarks. Shooting records tell us there had been thousands of grey partridges – eight-hundred-and-twenty were shot in one morning in 1935 – and in the 1700s hundreds of hares sustained the daily hare-coursing."

But by the 1980s hares, grey partridges and other once common birds had become rarities. "Field sizes expanded from thirty to three-hundred acres, and miles of hedgerows were ripped out. I saw sprayed fields full of flailing birds in their death throes," says Peter. "Across the country ancient woodlands, wetlands, chalk grasslands and rivers were destroyed. We realised too late that birds had disappeared with them."

Although hedgerows and woodland were conserved at Courtyard, the decline in wildlife was not reversed until Peter went organic. Since then brown hares, skylarks and grey partridges have increased up to five-fold. Badgers, woodpeckers and turtle doves have returned after decades of absence. Predatory buzzards, marsh harriers and barn owls signal a replenished ecosystem, but Peter still has concerns: "Their territories stretch way beyond our eight hundred and ninety acres, and neighbouring farms are not organic.

"Since World War Two, food and farming has careered in one direction and farms, machinery and commercial interests have become bigger and bigger. But the juggernaut is shuddering to a halt. We know that industrialised food is making us sick, some sprays are being banned, and the fuel on which it all runs is becoming more expensive. One of our workers remembers the first pesticide sprayer – horse-drawn! – and has lived to see the last. We'll look back on this period as a tiny but destructive blip in the history of agriculture.

Pupils from Docking Primary School come to feed animals, visit pig arks, picnic among straw bales and grind wheat to make chocolate chip biscuits. "I want them to understand the connection between the fields they see and the food they eat, between pigs and sausages, cows and burgers. Children at Docking understand more than most because what they do here creates a buzz in the playground," says Peter.

Despite the catering industry's notorious inertia, he expects all schools will eventually adopt the Food for Life standard, which sets minimums for fresh, seasonal, local and organic ingredients and requires food and cooking education. "It just takes parental or public pressure and a few well-publicised examples. I've seen resistant local authorities transform into ambassadors," he says.

"Now is an incredibly exciting time of change. Organic agriculture can protect wildlife and provide enough food," says Peter. "Because it restores the soil, it reduces carbon emissions and is more flood and drought resistant. Imagine the impact if all of Britain went organic."

Titchwell Manor

Main Road Titchwell King's Lynn
Norfolk PE31 8BB
01485 210221 www.titchwellmanor.com

Cromer crab with beetroot, rosewater and yogurt sorbet? Lavender custard with caramelised white chocolate and nutmeg lollipop? While many chefs who focus on local and seasonal ingredients keep dishes traditional, Eric Snaith can't help but follow his imagination and his Norfolk larder is treated to an innovative workout.

The setting is classic: a tall redbrick Victorian farmhouse, minutes by foot from the coast, with walled garden, high ceilings and lofty conservatory dining room. Black and white photos of family beach scenes float on walls like childhood memories, while ceiling fans and potted ferns lend a colonial air. Eric's parents Margaret and Ian bought the hotel in 1988 so Eric considers himself a Norfolk lad.

"I started helping out washing pots as a teenager, then assisting the chefs, and discovered I had a knack for cooking. So after travelling the world I came home to take over the reins. Working for a family business is great as I'm free to choose our suppliers and experiment in the kitchen, which gives me a real buzz."

Eric pairs classic flavour combinations with one or two surprises, then applies inventive techniques to vary textures: seared dived scallops with compressed cucumber (dehydrated to intensify colour and flavour), cucumber salsa, fried capers and caper powder; Berkshire pork two ways – confit belly that's cooked eighteen hours sous vide (partially cooked, then vacuum sealed to intensify flavour) then caramelised, and pink tenderloin – with crackling, smoked mashed potato croquettes and fennel three ways. Chocolate tart is matched with black olives and fennel ice cream.

Increasingly, customers are willing to be adventurous. His inspired ice creams and sorbets are hugely popular – liquorice, chestnut, rose, tonka bean, parsnip and honey, Earl Grey – echoing the eighteenth-century British fashion for exotic flavours.

There is plenty of tamer fare, including the bar menu: smoked salmon with crème fraîche and cornichons; soused mackerel with cucumber and capers; deep fried haddock with mushy peas and chips; chargrilled ribeye with pepper and brandy butter.

And of course, there are rock oysters on ice, dressed crabs and steaming pots of mussels and hand-racked cockles from third generation local shellfish veteran, Cyril Southerland.

"Hand-raked cockles are much harder work than dredged but they're much better, and so Cyril gets his son to do it. Those tubs of little nude cockles you see in shops and stalls all over Norfolk were most likely dredged, which smashes up their shells and disturbs the seabed, and have been to Holland and back for processing. I'll only buy Cyril's, which are intact and never frozen," says Eric.

Local fishermen, who use day-boats, lines and nets off the shore, supply sea bass, skate, flounder and Dover sole. Eric will no longer buy cod or wild salmon as their Atlantic stocks are threatened. Rare breed beef, lamb and venison come from the Norfolk estates of Sandringham, Houghton Hall and Holkham, including a cured and air-dried lamb similar to the Norwegian speciality fenalår which Eric serves with beetroot and celeriac rémoulade. Pork comes from the FruitPig Company, based the other side of Kings Lynn, who source rare breed, pedigree, free-range pork from local smallholdings.

"Matt Cockin is so passionate about his pork. If it's not good enough he won't supply it, whereas many other butchers would send it anyway to make the money. He makes fantastic pancetta, prosciutto-style ham, black pudding and sausages, all of which come with the pig's breed, birth and slaughter date on the label," enthuses Eric, who treasures his relationship with local suppliers.

Eric is also a keen forager, whether it's in his mother's garden for nasturtiums, pansies and marigolds to garnish salads, in the next door vegetable patch for courgette flowers, herbs and raspberries or along the coast for sea beet, sea purslane and marsh samphire. "Others pass so much by, like banks of elderflowers, wild fennel and blackberries."

Once a term forty small children crocodile their way from the local school to Titchwell Manor for lunch. "We cook things they're unlikely to eat at home and present it beautifully to tempt them. We talk about where ingredients come from, how they're cooked and healthy eating. They're always fascinated by stories from our staff – a young crowd of South Africans, Australians, Eastern Europeans and Jamaicans – and we hope to provide a real window on the world for them."

Titchwell Manor

Evening main courses £12–£23
Weekday 2-course set lunch from £12
Food always available
Nearest train: Kings Lynn

Woodlands Farm

Kirton House Boston
Lincolnshire PE20 1JD
01205 724778 www.woodlandsfarm.co.uk

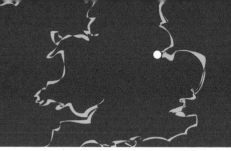

A statue of William Dennis, the 'Potato King', stands outside Kirton town hall, honouring the pioneer who supplied potatoes to feed all of London's poor at King Edward VII's Coronation feast of 1902. Today his great-grandson, Andrew Dennis, farms the same tract of Lincolnshire fens. He still uses the 'chitting' technique (sprouting potatoes in light) that his ancestor developed. But in his hands Woodlands Farm has been transformed and now wins acclaim for a multitude of vegetables, woodland turkeys, rare Lincolnshire breeds and an award-winning organic box scheme. In 2009 Andrew was voted BBC Radio 4's Farmer of the Year.

"My responsibility is to nurture the land and ensure its health for future generations," he says. "When I took over, Woodlands was intensively farmed to supply supermarkets, like many local farms. But I'd noticed fewer gulls following the plough which is a sign of disappearing earthworms, and pesticides and chemicals were polluting the dykes. The ecosystem was suffering." When a dog was poisoned from drinking a puddle, it was the last straw. Andrew began the conversion to organic of all seventeen-hundred acres.

"I'm interested in 'connectedness', in bridging the gap between town and farm so that people come to develop an affection for the land. We've opened to the public and run educational and cultural programmes. People come to collect eggs, pick strawberries and even help pack our veg boxes. It's a pity when people think of farms as unapproachable. They can be sources of enormous interest and pleasure."

On the Poetry Trail visitors contemplate verse attached to grain dryers and cauliflower planters; local schools run poetry and art competitions inspired by the farm; painters and musicians gather for workshops. Supermarket sales are down to forty per cent and a box scheme means they know their customers.

The monks of Crowland Abbey reclaimed this land – known as South Holland – nine hundred years ago. The fertile soil benefited from millennia of tidal deposits and it is ideal for the cultivation of vegetables; Andrew's pointed cabbages stole the show at the organic produce awards, beating many exotic competitors.

There are purple, white and green cauliflowers, sweetcorn, carrots with names like Atomic Red, Cosmic Purple and Mellow Yellow (orange carrots were a seventeenth-century invention), heirloom tomatoes, lilac aubergines, artichokes, asparagus, rhubarb, melons and raspberries. Whereas his predecessors cultivated just one potato – Maris Pipers for chips – Andrew successfully grows a dozen varieties.

Andrew watches the three-hundred acres of his new biodynamic farming pilot project like a hawk. Soil and plants are treated, at specific times of day, with homeopathic tonics; his experienced growers were amazed to find their first biodynamic cabbages unusually healthy and weed-free. They are sold with the Demeter certification logo.

"Biodynamic is sometimes known as 'organic plus'. It sees farms as living organisms with individual identities which their crops inherit. I'm quite content not to understand how it all works," says Andrew. "It's rewarding and fun to preserve some of nature's wonder."

Indigenous livestock has reappeared at Woodlands: slow-growing Lincolnshire Red cattle; shaggy Lincoln Longwool sheep, whose billowing fleeces built the local wool trade, funding the six church spires seen from the farm; scarlet-plumed Lincolnshire Buff chickens, who grow slowly for eight months. Their meat is available by mail-order.

The Lincolnshire Curly Coat pig became extinct in 1972 so Andrew acquired Gavin and Stacey, two wavy-haired Hungarian Mangalitzas, a breed that is similar and under threat. He brought in traditional Bronze and Black Norfolk turkeys, too, who strut happily under trees and, with unclipped wings, can express their natural instinct to perch on boughs.

"Turkeys are sometimes abused by modern farming, with thousands to a shed," says Andrew whose pioneering approach has helped improve turkey welfare across the country. "We slaughter them one by one, out of sight of others. The challenge is to afford the birds dignity in death as well as in life."

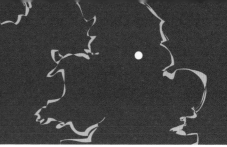

Stichelton Dairy
Collingthwaite Farm Cuckney Mansfield
Nottinghamshire NG20 9NP
01623 844883 www.stichelton.co.uk

Britain was once teeming with cheesemakers: in the 1930s over sixteen-hundred farms were making it. By the early nineties that number had dwindled to one-hundred, due to post-war industrialisation of cheese-making, supermarkets driving demand for mass-produced cheese and food safety concerns. The number is creeping up again, though, and Joe Schneider – "an American who started out making Greek cheese for a Turk in Holland" – is part of the renaissance.

Over a pint in 2004 Randolph Hodgson of Neal's Yard Dairy planted the idea in Joe's mind of recreating raw milk Stilton, which had disappeared in 1989 due to unproven health scares. Randolph sells the best cheeses, works closely with makers to improve their techniques and advises government on dairy issues.

When the name Stilton was protected by European law in 1996, the 'Protected Designation of Origin' (PDO) stated pasteurised milk should be used, despite it having nothing to do with traditional methods. One could infer this ruling protects industry more than traditional food.

So, although Joe is making a cheese that is faithful to the traditional Stilton recipe, he can't call it Stilton for he is using raw milk. His milk is from a single organic herd: one-hundred-and-fifty Friesian-Holstein cows at Collingthwaite Farm on the Wellbeck estate in Nottinghamshire. 'Stichelton' was the original name for the village of Stilton, a staging post on the Great North Road where farmhouse cheeses were brought to be sold.

"Mick Lingard, the herdsman, has managed cows for fifty years, since he was eight," says Joe. "He'd been highly sceptical about the idea of going organic, but once over the teething problems he said it was like being reborn."

Joe's cheese reflects its natural herbaceous origins and even the passing seasons, just as a good wine expresses its terroir. "It's like a single malt," he explains. This direct connection to the cows, and ultimately the soil, allows Joe to make cheese that is safe.

In France and Italy, too, raw milk cheeses such as Comté, Camembert and Parmesan are made in quantity with confidence because each batch of single-herd milk will be consistent. By contrast, Stilton-makers mix milks so there is little option but to pasteurise. "It's an unknown, so it's treated like liquid poison," says Joe.

His aim was to create the creamy cheese with cool blue notes and touches of syrupy sweetness that Randolph had lodged in his memory. To achieve it he ladles the delicate curds by hand and later 'rubs up' with knives to seal the cheeses. He makes forty tonnes a year, compared to the six-thousand tonnes of Stilton that is sold. Joe is continually tweaking his recipe. "Sometimes I feel like a blind man with Randolph saying 'a bit to the right, a bit to the left.'" One leap forward was made by switching from commercial starter (the bacteria added to acidify the milk and contribute flavour and texture) to one used in the eighties. This complex blend of bacterial strains, some unidentified, had miraculously been saved and kept alive for eighteen years. The results were astounding.

And using raw milk, with billions of living micro-organisms, magnifies the taste. "You can still feel the flavours rolling round in your mouth several minutes later, like the finish on a fine wine," says Joe.

The alchemy of turning mild white milk into such complexity of flavour, texture and colour has fascinated us for millennia. To create Stichelton, tiny amounts of rennet set the curds, as they would in a calf's stomach, the starter weaves its bacterial magic, and penicillium roqueforti blooms into blue-green veins. Until the Stichelton is pierced, it is dry, crumbly and acidic; activated by air, the mould interacts with proteins and fats creating that buttery texture. Over three months a rind forms, and cheesemaker, then affineur, watches like a hawk and manipulates temperature and humidity. As one noted Edwardian Stilton-maker remarked, "… stiltons are more trouble than babies."

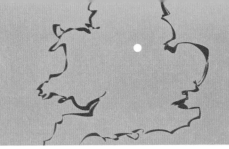

Langar Hall

Church Lane Langar Nottingham
Nottinghamshire NG13 9HG
01949 860559 www.langarhall.com

Imogen Skirving was an early convert to 'slow food'. Back in the nineties, when she made the decision to take Langar Hall down the country house hotel path, she asked local farmers if they would supply their meat direct, so she wouldn't have to suffer the vagaries of quality and provenance that she'd experienced with wholesale market suppliers. It took a few years, and the acquisition of a like-minded head chef, to persuade the farmers this was a good business move. As Imogen says: "We're privileged to have such a fund of food around us and I wanted to use it. It probably costs me more – we employ an extra chef to do the butchering – but it's worth it for the quality and freshness."

Set in private parkland in the Vale of Belvoir, south-east of Nottingham on the Leicestershire border, a good proportion of Langar Hall's produce comes from within a twenty-mile radius. The local farmshop at Clipston supplies veal, beef and poultry; pork, duck, Stilton and hen eggs come from nearby Colston Bassett. She is "scandalised" by the poor quality of fish that some large suppliers try to send her; finding a reliable fish supplier when you're in the country and far away from a coastline is a challenge, although she has a constant supply of very good Scottish shellfish. Their lamb is reared on the estate and Imogen is happy that they enjoy a stress-free life grazing on the old pasture around the house.

Bill and Harry are her two septuagenarian gardeners (both ex-miners); Bill has gamekeeper friends who ensure Langar's kitchens get the seasonal pick of the partridges, pheasants, rabbits, hares and pigeons. Damsons come from one of the keepers' gardens; mirabelles (small golden plums) come free from a tree in the village; customers bring walnuts, blackberries and mushrooms (including Nottinghamshire blewits), as gifts or in exchange for meals.

Bill and Harry keep the restaurant well-supplied with salad crops, soft fruits, herbs and vegetables. "Guests love to walk around the beds admiring the produce and knowing they will eat it later," says Imogen. It cannot supply all their needs though and Imogen has to "import" from Lincolnshire. "But I get furious if I have to go abroad. I absolutely try and keep to the UK. If we can't get something fresh, we change the menu. The only exception is frozen peas because the quality is good, and I've served my time pea-podding!"

Imogen was brought up at Langar Hall, a quintessential Georgian, English country house: small but perfectly formed and set at the end of a magical avenue of lime trees. A love of food and cooking, and a particular passion for Elizabeth David, lead her to London's Cordon Bleu school before a career in fine art galleries and art restoration. After her father died, Imogen intended to continue running the Hall as a guesthouse for a short

while before selling it. "But I was working so hard, I didn't have time to think about selling. And I loved building relationships with the guests."

Menus are a collaboration between Imogen and her young, local, loyal and enthusiastic chefs and they always reflect the character of Langar. "A chef once said to me: 'Food must mirror the place where it is served; it must be sympathetic.' Our menus wouldn't work in the centre of a city and city restaurant menus wouldn't work here." In winter game terrine, roast wood pigeon and damson soufflé are on the menu; in summer a trio of Langar lamb and iced raspberry parfait. Langar's twice-baked cheese soufflé, one of their most popular dishes, remains on the menu throughout the year.

Langar Hall revolves around its restaurant, and many customers drive up to fifty miles for Sunday lunch or an evening out. "I'm told people find it a sort of sanctuary," says Imogen. "The countryside around Nottingham is quite plain and flat, then you turn into this avenue of lime trees and you're in another world." The small, pillared dining room manages to be both elegant and relaxing; crisp cloths, chandeliers and gilt-framed paintings combine with dreamy views over parkland and pasture.

There's no formality – "it doesn't register with me whether guests are in jeans or dinner jackets," says Imogen – and there's a tangible sense of time slowing down. It's not unusual for Sunday lunchers to linger over coffee until early evening; unless it's a very busy Saturday evening, tables are rarely booked twice.

Langar is imbued with Imogen's personality: warm, engaging, idiosyncratic, empathetic, but nobody's fool. She might be manning the bar or answering the telephone or chatting with customers but she is also in and out of the kitchen, tasting and testing and even pot-washing. And she's constantly thinking of ways to keep quality high and costs low. Her latest idea to process kitchen waste is to buy a pig.

Langar Hall

Evening main courses £12.50–£22.50
Best meal deal: Sun/Mon eve 2/3 course £20/£25
Food served 12–2 and 6.30–9.30 daily
Nearest train: Nottingham

The George

Alstonefield Ashbourne
Staffordshire DE6 2FX 01335 310205
www.thegeorgeatalstonefield.com

When Emily Hammond returned from London to take over the family pub in Staffordshire's Peak District, it might have looked a simple task. She grew up in The George, knew the place inside out, knew, and was known by, the locals. However, all those things made it harder. "I wanted it to remain a pub that has a place in people's hearts," she says, "but I knew I had to build something to appeal to a wider audience and I wanted to put good, local, seasonal food at its heart."

Trying to achieve both goals, since she took charge in 2005, has been tricky, particularly in a small village where there are inevitable comparisons with former landlords.

Emily's solution has been to do everything slowly and subtly and to make sure the villagers and newcomers are

uncluttered with polished floorboards, scrubbed pine tables, pots of flowers gathered from the kitchen garden and plain white china.

The monthly-changing menu still has sandwiches made with ham that has been home-baked for eight hours, a Walker's Platter of soup and sandwiches, hand-raised steak and ale pie, Spotted Dick. But these are mixed with modern dishes: buffalo mozzarella with roast beetroot; gammon steak with fried duck's egg and pineapple chutney; sourdough bread with dressed Devon crab; seared scallops in borlotti and chestnut soup; star anise and pear bread and butter pudding. "It's simple and seasonal with a twist," she says.

Everything, except bread, is made in-house, including

happy. So, the front bar is relatively unchanged with its Georgian tiled floor, old village photographs, polished brasses and the regulars' tankards hanging behind the gleaming copper-topped bar; walkers are welcome and dogs can still flop in the bar.

The dining area – "I remind people who call it a restaurant that we are a pub," Emily says – is light and

the ice cream, sorbets, elderberry chutney and lemonade. The pub would bake its own bread, says Emily, but old pub kitchens are small and make it difficult to control the temperature of the yeast. Apart from fish and seafood, virtually everything is sourced locally. "All the fish we buy is Marine Stewardship Council-certified and all, apart from the prawns, comes from British waters." Wootton

Organic supplies beef, lamb, chicken and venison. Much of their soft fruit and vegetables are grown in the pub's kitchen garden, formerly a campsite and another example of Emily's careful 'upgrading'.

"It's been a steep learning curve," she admits. "I soon realised we can't grow enough potatoes but we're pretty sufficient in things like beans, cabbages, carrots, courgettes, herbs and beetroot."

Kitchen waste is used for compost and Emily employs a local couple to tend the garden. She uses two local businesses, one a market gardener, for additional supplies and only resorts to imports for citrus fruits and out-of-season tomatoes and salad garnishes. "You will never see air-freighted fine beans on our menu, though," she says.

Tuesday and Friday nights, a band of locals gather to drink and chat late into the night. "Conversation flows easily from one table to the next and walkers or fishermen share their stories." There's no sense of newcomers being excluded and there are cribbage, dominoes and guide books for all to share.

Emily stocks household essentials in the farmshop and takes newspaper orders, too. She has also created work enough for three full-time chefs and seventeen other part-time staff. All of that is quite an achievement, yet perhaps Emily is most pleased that she has managed to hold on to the 'pubbiness' of The George.

"There's a convivial atmosphere," says Emily proudly. "We're still an institution."

Whatever is in season, and local, is in the farmshop across the courtyard. Emily could have converted it into bedrooms but felt there were enough holiday options for visitors already and, instead, has made it something for the community: a shop with a party space above; her first booking was for a village wedding.

The local cricket team still meets at the pub and, on

The George

Evening main courses £10–£20
Wines £12–£27
Toast and dripping by the fire
Nearest train: Derby/Matlock

North England

Location

Key

- Alastair Sawday's Special Places to eat
- Soil Association certified organic producers

Map 5

North England

Unicorn

89 Albany Road Chorlton
Manchester M21 0BN
01618 617675 www.unicorn-grocery.co.uk

Unicorn's one-stop shop with nearly four thousand lines is re-inventing the supermarket. "I know four thousand is nothing compared to a supermarket's usual twenty-five thousand," founder Adam York says, "but their duplication of items only offers an illusion of choice. And most of it is reliant on cheap labour, cheap fuel and a globalised food system which is often unfair to producers in developing countries."

Unicorn, a worker co-operative, sources direct from producers, buying in bulk where possible, packing into smaller bags on-site. Costs associated with a complex food-chain involving multiple depots, packing sites and thousands of motorway miles, are avoided. Unicorn places great importance on sourcing affordable, wholesome food that provides secure and equitable employment for those who produced or processed it. When you enter under the wide awning, emblazoned with the words 'eat your greens', you'll find vegetables and fruit sourced as locally as possible, all kinds of dried wholefoods – from blackeye beans to farro – deli treats cooked on-site and fresh bread. Most is organic, much fairtrade.

"When our doors opened in September 1996 customers poured in, and still do." Now over forty members own and staff the business and the turnover is several million. "Our customers are very food literate, and we provide information so they can make informed choices. We're welcoming to all and competitive on prices," says Adam.

In 2001 he helped found a market garden, Glebelands, two miles away in Sale, to grow salads and greens for Unicorn. So Unicorn's customers get super-fresh produce; the same leaves from southern Spain use twenty-six times the transport fuel.

"There's all this talk about eating wonderful local, seasonal food, but British horticulture is in disarray and needs support. So we work hard to build relationships with growers by offering expertise, paying on time and giving practical help." During the disastrously sodden summers of 2007 and 2008, Unicorn made 'wet weather payments' to its suffering growers to show solidarity. "The government wouldn't have cared if they'd floated out to sea," he says.

Unicorn's pay structure is flat, and there is a culture of consensual decision-making. "We want members to be highly involved," says Adam. He believes Unicorn generates more money for the community through wages, per square foot of premises, than supermarkets. "We're proud that our pounds circulate locally; chain

supermarket profits end up in a few hands." Five per cent of total payroll is donated to community food projects for people suffering the iniquities of world trade.

"Ideas happen at Unicorn," says member Rob Alderson. "For example the 'living roof' project, which created over eight-hundred-square meters of habitats on the flat roof to increase biodiversity."

Rob has been instrumental in Unicorn's new Glazebury project: the acquisition of twenty-one fertile acres west of Manchester to create a sustainable model for feeding the city in the face of uncertainties about oil. Unicorn raised capital via Loanstock, a fixed, five-year investment with fixed rate of return on the investment. "So many customers invested in Loanstock, it's humbling and really makes us want to do a good job." Rob and fellow Unicorn member Stu have sown vetch to build soil fertility before growing leeks, spinach, celery and cabbage.

"It's a beautiful site, with amazing sunsets," says Rob, who is determined the only carbon emissions will come from a little tractor diesel; wind and sunshine will provide energy, a borehole the water.

Adam maintains there is still masses of work to be done. "There are little food initiatives here and there, but still those worse off are eating poorly and it'll be business as usual until the price of oil seriously rises. Then when the high streets that were destroyed and the farms that were abandoned can't just bounce back, people will realise the disaster of what is happening."

Pipe & Glass Inn

West End South Dalton Beverley
Yorkshire HU17 7PN
01430 810246 www.pipeandglass.co.uk

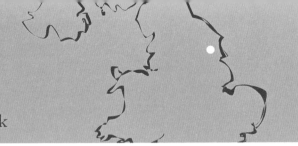

When James Mackenzie and his wife Kate came across the Pipe and Glass Inn in 2006 it was trading badly. "Its heyday had been twenty odd years ago," explains James, "but we sensed that it still held a warm place in people's hearts."

They were right. The pub, a gatehouse to Dalton Park, is seventeenth century and has parkland views. "One of the reasons for our success is that people who came here as children, in the days when all the kids were outside with coke and crisps, have come back with their children."

James and Kate have kept the pub's dark furniture, spindle-back chairs and copper warming pans but there are olives on the bar next to the pickled eggs, hand-pulled beers and fat candles on the tables. The dining area has chunky Chesterfields around a wood-burning stove, recycled oak tables, wooden settles and polished floors.

James was brought up to appreciate good food and food provenance; his mum was a talented cook, one granny was a baker, the other lived on a farm. He remembers "eviscerating chickens and standing on chairs to help with cooking". After stints in various kitchens he became head chef at The Star Inn in North Yorkshire, one of Britain's first pubs to be awarded a Michelin star. "The chef-patron, Andrew Pern, and I knew each other from college days. We held the same values." After three years of enjoyable graft as The Star's reputation grew, James and Kate wanted to find their own place.

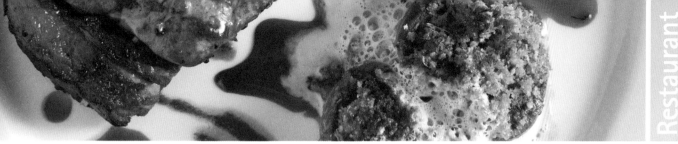

James dislikes the term gastropub but admits it's useful if it indicates a place that cares about its food. "At the Pipe & Glass we're about 'real' food and staff are trained to think about every stage of preparation. I point out that the farmer has cared for the product so they have to care for it, too. The best ingredients need little intervention from a chef."

"Our suppliers know that we need consistency. Occasionally if something is local but inferior, I won't use it. I'll use certain vegetables from France and Longhorn beef comes from Ross-on-Wye in Herefordshire."

Lamb comes from a local shepherd and his wife who do their own butchering; he gets a Gloucester Old Spot pig delivered every other week and the kitchen uses every part; game comes from local estates; vegetables and herbs are largely local (such as Pickering watercress and Sand Hutton asparagus); fish is from the local coast. "Keith, an ex-fisherman, runs Coral Reef, a small wet fish shop at Hornsea, and he'll get me lobsters and crabs or smoked haddock from Carnaby near Bridlington, or just tell me what he thinks is best and turn up with it. He and his wife enjoy eating here." James enjoys food for free, too, and has masses of wild garlic in his garden and nettles, elderberries and puffball mushrooms.

James describes his cooking as "gutsy but refined". He is not fond of jellies and foams unless they are playing an important part in the taste. He is undoubtedly skilful – the pub has a Michelin Bib Gourmand – and enjoys using less popular fish or cuts of meat and being imaginative with them. He might take two lamb bellies, roll them together, braise for five hours then pan-fry and serve with little faggots and a nettle and mint sauce; grilled mackerel might come on a bed of samphire and the fish pie might surprise with its 'Scarborough woof'. He only buys fish that is caught sustainably.

James is a great believer in recognising limitations. "Why make sausages if someone else can make them better?" His supplier, James White, a butcher at nearby Hutton Cranswick, has doubled his sausage sales since the pub has spread his reputation. Bread is from a local baker who makes spelt, walnut, and parsnip and parmesan breads just for James.

There are now around thirty-five staff, including eight chefs, yet James and Kate strive to keep things personal: staff visit local farms and breweries so they can enthuse about their products to customers, regulars' preferences are noted and remembered and they try to keep prices down. "If we've got Dover sole, we'll keep the price under £20 and not make much on it but I'd rather people went away happy and returned."

Pipe & Glass Inn

Evening main courses £10–£20
No food on Sunday eves or Mondays
(excluding bank holidays)
Nearest train: Beverley

Swillington Organic Farm

Swillington Leeds
Yorkshire LS26 8QA 0113 2869129
www.swillingtonorganicfarm.co.uk

At weekends the two-hundred-and-fifty-year-old walled garden is alive with the sounds of volunteers young and old tending a cornucopia of vegetables and fruits. The members of Swillington Farm's Community Supported Agriculture (CSA) scheme each pay an annual fee to share in the farm's produce.

Although they don't have to dedicate time to the growing themselves, each week many of them come and are addicted to their trips to the farm just outside Leeds.

Jo Cartwright, the owner of the land and the farmer, welcomes such passion and involvement.

"The idea of CSAs is to connect people to farms and to the land. People want to know where their food comes from and how it was grown, and many don't want to just eat the fruits but want to feel part of the process."

In the 1950s, Jo's father bought dilapidated stables on Swillington estate that for centuries was owned by the Lowther dynasty. They converted the stables into a farmhouse and acquired adjacent parkland as it became available.

Jo's love of wildlife and farm animals began then and she was destined to farm the land in her parents' footsteps.

"The farm's always been mixed, which makes life much more interesting and disease control easier," says Jo. Aberdeen Angus cattle, native sheep, Saddleback pigs, goats, chickens and ducks are rotated to avoid problems with pests and disease.

In the interests of conservation, Jo converted to organic farming and encouraged wildlife through hedge and tree planting, coppicing and reed bed management.

The diverse habitats – great avenues of lime trees, marshland, pasture, ponds and woodland – attract harvest mice, red kites, owls, waders and more.

Meat, garden produce, eggs and honey are sold at the farm shop (Thursdays to Saturdays), at farmers' markets and to several CSA groups around Leeds. Mail order will be available in the future.

The public is welcomed on open days, and groups book special tours. Jo is planning a kitchen so schoolchildren can learn to grow, harvest, cook and then eat their food, all onsite. "And we have big events for CSA members: scarecrow-making in spring and hog roasts and barn dances in autumn. The volunteer committee organises them all," says Jo.

It used to be a half-day trek to the slaughterhouse. Frustrated, Jo built a processing room, where she swiftly dispatches fifty chickens a week. Sheep and pigs now travel just three miles. "The more local the better: less cost, fuel and pollution. I hated being stuck on the M62 when I could be farming. And there's less stress for the animals, which produces better meat."

Ian Richardson, Jo's butcher, prepares whatever customers want. "We use the whole animal: bones for stock, retired laying hens for chicken soup, lamb's neck for stews, pig liver, heart, spare ribs, ham hocks, belly and cheek." Jo used to butcher all her own meat "Until," she says, "the novelty of farming during daylight hours and butchering by night wore off."

Most eighteenth-century country houses had kitchen gardens, where walls protected an astounding array of fruits and vegetables from wind, frost and nibbling rabbits. During World War I most fell into disuse as the legions of workers required to keep them productive and sound were required for the war effort. "They fell into disuse which is such a shame. You see some used as car-parks in houses and farms open to the public. They ought to be growing food," says Jo.

She is renovating the crumbling walls of her own two-acre garden brick by brick. Pigs, employed as rotivators, snuffled out the remains of Victorian piping that was used to heat the soil. "The lowliest gardener's job would have been tending the fires and flues, which heated the wall cavities," she explains.

Fig, peach and apricot trees thrive against the south-facing wall. Polytunnels, bought with CSA profits, grow salad leaves year-round, including mizuna, amaranth and mustards. "I'd love to rebuild the glasshouses, where they'd have once grown pineapples. I like growing a bit of everything and constantly experimenting," says Jo, who is enthusiastically aided by organic apprentice, Kate Edwards, and resident goat-farmer and CSA champion, Kirstin Glendinning.

CSA members share both the rewards and risks of farming. So when blight destroyed the tomato plants, members scurried for their green tomato chutney recipes. And when harvests seemed never-ending, Kirstin threw a Jerusalem artichoke party for fans of the sweet, knobbly tuber. Members weigh out their shares in the shed and take only what they need, or swap, so waste is minimal.

"It requires more effort from customers, but it's excellent value. Our shares are considerably cheaper than supermarket equivalents, and of course are picked fresh, with zero food miles," says Jo, who also supplies chicken and pork to several other groups.

Aside from obvious benefits – an assured income for Jo and reasonably priced, farm-fresh food for consumers – the CSA has other far-reaching effects. Members love the collective effort and share their stories, thus spreading the word. Some have been inspired to start their own allotments, one created the website, another promotional videos, someone writes the newsletter and when it's all hands on deck, volunteers always pull their weight. "It has to be better than trekking food half-way round the world," insists Jo. "and it's good preparation for the time when we will have to be more self-sufficient."

The Traddock

Austwick Settle
Yorkshire LA2 8BY
01524 251224 www.thetraddock.co.uk

The dramatic ancient landscape of the Yorkshire Dales National Park shoots off in all directions from this Georgian country house and Bruce and Jane Reynolds have made it their mission to offer guests the friendliest place from which to enjoy a real taste of the countryside. This is a family enterprise: son Paul and wife Jenny have joined the team; daughters Sacha and Katie have also helped out.

Jane and chef John Pratt share a passion for "wholesome, old fashioned, 'slow' cooking", which uses artisan produce, reflects the region's culinary heritage and is lovingly made from scratch. "I remember when people only bought food from the local butcher, baker and greengrocer. But supermarkets have risen to dominate all, peddling the bland flavours and inferior products which so many people now accept," says Jane. "When people come here, they taste the difference."

The Reynolds lived in Africa for twenty-five years, when Bruce was in banking. Jane tells how the taste of chicken bought there made her realise how much was being lost back home. "Real chicken is almost gamey, due to a natural diet and outdoor exercise, and supermarket chicken tastes of very little. I've seen factory farms and now we only buy free-range and organic poultry from Lowther Park and Swillington farms."

Kitchen stalwart, Rosie Wakeman, makes breads, muffins, biscuits and shortbread, and creates pickles, chutneys, jams, jellies and curds. The hotel's award-winning breakfasts include her homemade smoothies, compôtes, granola, croissants and marmalade, alongside

smoked salmon with scrambled eggs, smoked haddock with poached egg, porridge with cream and the full English with organic black pudding from Bumpy Lane Farm. Much of the food here is organic, including half the seventy-strong wine list and a number of beers, ciders and whiskies.

"Organic food has a lower carbon footprint and usually tastes better. The difference between organic and conventional tomatoes is phenomenal, one reason why we're going to grow our own." Once Jane's children berated her for sending them to school with embarrassing homemade brown bread and flapjacks, now they feed their own small children nothing but organic food.

Organic meat comes from Jim Hadwin at Mansergh Hall near Kirkby Lonsdale or Roy Porter, a traditional

Butcher at Chatburn near Clitheroe, milk and cream from Low Sizergh Farm (see page 166) in neighbouring Cumbria, and vegetables from Growing with Grace (see page 162) two miles up the road. This community farm produces heirloom varieties specifically for The Traddock and in spring they give Jane leaves to create a 'wild weed salad' from chickweed, dandelion, pennycress, oxalis, hairy bittercress, fat hen and garlic mustard.

Chef John hunts down old cookbooks and wartime Women's Institute magazines for recipes, then adds a nod to twenty-first century style: Gloucester Old Spot pork belly with spectacular crackling cooked for hours in spiced apple juice and served with vanilla-scented mash and red cabbage; meltingly tender Saddleback pork cheeks braised in dark ale with prunes; locally shot pigeon galantine with chestnut stuffing made to an eighteenth-century recipe; rolled ribeye beef Wellington with girolles. "Many old recipes use cheaper cuts and are very relevant today."

An advocate of the Slow Food movement and its emphasis on regionality, John is adding more traditional north-west specialities to the menu such as Yorkshire pikelets, Lancashire hotpot with pickled red cabbage and spiced parkin. An annual project with local schools sees children developing seasonal, organic, Yorkshire menus under his guidance, with winning recipes making it onto the Traddock's menu for a month. John is also planning Slow Food events to showcase his artisan suppliers. "The Slow Food movement is a boost and gives them the recognition they deserve, especially important when they cannot afford organic certification."

Jane says: "We're now drawing our sourcing net even closer to home. We value local artisan producers above all. They challenge the hegemony of the supermarkets and we want to support that."

The Traddock

Evening main courses £13.50–£17.95
Best meal deal: 3-course lunch £16.95
Regular food and wine tasting evenings
Nearest train: Settle

Martina Myerscough's Damascene moment came on a Friday night, late 2004, in torrential rain stuck in London's traffic. She rang her boss, handed in her notice, drove five hours home to Liverpool and announced to husband Jonathan: "I've done my bit of the bargain, now it's your turn!"

Six months later (after Jonathan had obligingly sold his golfing business) they opened the Red Pump Inn, a Grade II-listed former coaching inn, near Clitheroe in Lancashire. Garnering awards, a devoted clientele (who think nothing of driving an hour to find their lick-spit of a village) and a reputation for being decidedly different, they've had not a moment to look back.

Neither had any experience of the hospitality industry, other than as 'professional consumers'. "We are passionate foodies," explains Martina, who gave up a director-level job in the healthcare sector. "We are boringly obsessive about food. I grew up in a big family where it was a given that we sat down to supper each night." Jonathan's affection for food developed early and was inspired by his GP father who would dash home from

surgery in time to cook supper for his four children.

The more the Myerscoughs travelled with work, the more they ate out, the more they became disillusioned, both with their lifestyle and the eating-out experience. "We'd come away from a place feeling we'd been marketed to, not fed," says Martina. "Everything about the Red Pump – whether it's the food, the décor, the staff – had to appeal to us. It has to be somewhere we'd want to go: cosy, comfortable, chilled out and with the highest quality food."

That ninety-five per cent of their food is sourced locally simply makes sense, says Martina. "If an animal is reared well and needs only to travel a short distance to get here, I'm going to keep going back to the farmer that produced it. Our suppliers are small companies, like us, so we understand each other's challenges."

From the pub, overlooking the Ribble Valley and surrounded by six farms, they can virtually see their future supplies. Beef (aged for twenty-four to twenty-eight days) and pork come from Pendle Hill, lamb from the Trough of Bowland, game from the surrounding

moorland, vegetables from Clitheroe market, fish from nearby Morecambe and herbs from their own garden.

If locals have a glut of fruit or vegetables they exchange them for a couple of pints. (Two local brews, one regional, one national including one from Yorkshire, one from Lancashire to keep locals, in this border territory, happy.) On not a few occasions, Martina and Jonathan have been apprehended by the police as they scrambled down road embankments collecting wild garlic in April or hedgerow fruits in autumn.

Menus are a collaboration between suppliers, Martina and Jonathan, and their chefs. "A farmer might ring up and say: 'We've got some ox cheeks, would you like some?'" says Martina.

"Our style is rustic and flavoursome; we tend not to play about with food. It's not a big menu and everything is made to order." (The Myerscoughs are both good cooks and occasionally act as commis chefs.) And everything is made from scratch: bread, pasta, stocks, biscuits, preserves, puddings... even the fish is smoked themselves over a make-shift wok. The only thing Martina admits to not making is ice cream. "That comes from Uncle Bob at Chipping on Longridge Fell, a dairy farmer and butcher. It's absolutely fabulous!"

Every part of the animal is used, with bones and leftovers going into stocks, sauces and casseroles, and less popular, old-fashioned cuts – such as ox cheeks and brisket – reinvented and re-established. "All our food isn't necessarily slow to cook, but it does require time and commitment," explains Martina.

"Belly pork, jugged hare, marinated brisket – that takes seven days! When jugged hare is on – which is quite a faff to make, frankly – we have a special mailing list to alert customers."

Customers play a bigger role than perhaps people appreciate. The Red Pump's 'Rabbit Fest' dish, for example – a delicious slow confit of leg, pan-seared loin, rabbit haggis – came about because one customer said he liked all three ways of doing rabbit and found it hard to choose between them. "We couldn't do it on a massive scale but we can do it now and then for fun because we're small," explains Martina.

Actually, they're only small because they choose to

keep numbers down; their Slow food philosophy extends to leisurely, sociable eating. They never double-book tables (though they could sell them three times on Saturday evenings) with dining numbers averaging thirty to seventy, spread between the long galley, a handful of snugs with open fires and, if the weather's clement, the terrace. On the latter, guests are encouraged to pick up one of the Pump's blankets to keep warm.

The strict rules governing alterations to eighteenth-century, Grade II-listed properties made a wholesale switch to environmentally-friendly practices difficult but the Myerscoughs do what they can, conserving energy and water, reclaiming and restoring old furniture, recycling waste and distributing leftovers (not that there is much) to the local pigs.

The Myerscoughs pitch in where necessary to help their small, loyal (and local) staff – three in the kitchen, two to three waitresses – with Jonathan manning the bar, Martina front of house.

Chatting to customers is a vital part of the job. "We have a genuine interest in our guests and whether they like the food. Honest to God, I want to know if they didn't like something!" declares Martina.

She freely admits that they were considered mad when they opened. The Ribble valley is a foodie destination with several long-established and highly-regarded restaurants, so competition for the affections of diners is fierce. "We pitched up as novices. We don't have a big menu, we don't make a huge fuss about presentation, we're not frightened to do time-consuming dishes, we aren't striving to be full every night." She laughs at their naivety and their audaciousness before adding with a contented smile: "People can laugh all they like but we're having fun and our customers keep coming back."

Red Pump Inn

Evening main courses £8.95–£14.95
Best meal deal: 2-course lunch £12.95
No food Monday
Nearest train: Clitheroe

Growing With Grace

Clapham Nursery Clapham Lancaster
Lancashire LA2 8ER
01524 251723 www.growingwithgrace.co.uk

Neil Marshall is the co-founder of Growing with Grace, a small north Yorkshire co-operative run on Quaker principles of egalitarianism, spirituality and fairness. "At one time Quakers ran many big businesses – Barclays, Lloyds, Cadbury's, Rowntree's to name a few – and built their reputation on honesty and integrity. Nowadays many Quakers tend to look on the business world with rather a dim view. We wanted to demonstrate a different way of doing business: a social enterprise run as ethically as possible." Neil and wife Debby have been inspired, too, by Daily Bread, a Christian co-operative in the Midlands, and Scott Bader, a multinational chemical company operating under a workers' commonwealth.

In two acres of greenhouses Growing with Grace produces vegetables for the local community and supplies an organic shop, box scheme and farmers' market stalls with freshly picked vegetables, fruits, flowers and herbs.

Unaided by artificial heat or fertilisers, courgettes crop from mid-June to mid-October and mixed salad leaves are harvested year-round if the winter is mild. The most satisfying aspect for Neil is that the vegetables are grown on the local community's green waste. "It's a virtuous circle. Craven District Council delivers ten to eighteen tonnes of garden waste a week. We add nothing; it's very alive when it comes off the lorry. On the first night its temperature rises to 80°C. We inherited incredibly sterile soil, and the compost has transformed it. It works as mulch too, helping control weeds, and we think its dry, scratchy surface deters slugs," says Neil.

Plump Mediterranean aubergines, garlic, chillies, fennel and tomatoes thrive. Nasturtiums, borage, mallows and violas brighten popular mixed salad bags. Brassicas and legumes, not normally grown under glass, are rotated in to maintain healthy, fertile soil. In the 'forest garden' cherries, apricots, nectarines, figs, quinces and olives ripen

in succession while rhubarb, artichokes and cardoons sprawl in their shade and hops and grapevines climb above. "We're really hands-off with pests," says Neil. "Reacting to a small problem is normally unnecessary and rotation and diversity maintain health."

Growing with Grace enables Clapham village co-operative to recycle used cooking oil from restaurants and pubs into biodiesel that now fuels a number of villagers' cars. Profits are ploughed back into the community. A sustainable energy source is next: Neil wants to install a windmill and solar panels.

To complement their range and to top up out of season, the shop and box scheme source vegetables from Fold House Farm in Pilling and Stable Trading in Gisburn, eggs from Michael Pearson and mushrooms from Chris Thornborough in Poulton. Everything except the fairtrade chocolate swizzle sticks is organic.

"Fairtrade principles should be applied to struggling British farmers, too," says Neil. "And we need to remember in dealings globally, 'fairtrade' is not always fair when Western companies make the rules."

Neil grew up on a farm in Kenya and has memories of helping irrigate broad beans with recycled water. Later at agricultural college in England he researched the reclamation of land damaged by inappropriate farming in arid climates, and plotted his return to Africa. "But I realised we had a real problem right here, except that the damage we do is hidden because the climate's so forgiving: grass covers it up. In any other country our over-grazing would result in desertification."

Sticking to Quaker principles, all staff at Growing with Grace are paid equally. Neil remembers the split society and stark inequality back on the colonial Kenyan farm, and is adamant that at Growing with Grace, everyone, whether grower or decision-maker, should be valued equally and treated the same.

The Lunesdale Arms
Tunstall Carnforth
Lancashire LA6 2QN
01524 274203 www.thelunesdale.co.uk

Pop into the Lunesdale Arms on Tuesday and there'll be bridge players at one end, and pool players at the other. On Wednesday lunchtime a convivial group will be eating around a large table. On Thursday morning, the back bar doubles as the village Post Office with people stopping for a chat and a coffee. On Thursday evening a pianist works magic and on Sunday you'll stumble into a quiz. In December, if you time it right, you'll find the local Archdeacon retelling the Christmas story and encouraging everyone to belt out Christmas carols between their glasses of mulled wine.

Owner Emma Gillibrand says: "It's my aim that everyone should feel comfortable when they walk in." She bought the pub in 2001 and faced a huge challenge to banish the dusty pink anaglypta, mean little fires, high windows and dark rooms. Soon after opening foot-and-mouth brought the surrounding countryside to a halt.

She pressed on undeterred and revelled in the beauty of where she landed: "my kitchen has the best views of any restaurant kitchen!"

She always felt her venture would be a success. "In the Lune Valley there was virtually nowhere selling food that was homemade, locally sourced and, importantly, affordable." Her simple approach and high standards see customers beating a trail to her door.

The pub is a big, light, airy space of stripped floors, open beams, simple wooden tables, mismatched chairs, colourful modern art on white walls, and where the bar segues happily into the dining room. Big blue sofas sit around a wood-burning stove and there are newspapers and magazines. The menu, chalked on blackboards, changes almost daily – "except for the steak pie".

Emma buys as much locally as possible: lamb and pigs from Lune Valley farms, fish that's landed at Fleetwood and sausages and raised pork and black pudding pie from Mark at Dales butchers in Kirkby Lonsdale. Fruit, vegetables and organic salads leaves come from Lancashire growers. She chooses, though, to source her beef from Scotland and admits to occasionally using imported baby spinach leaves and fennel.

Some things she buys over the bar or in the village: "Someone came into the post office with masses of blackberries and apples and, a few weeks ago, I bought eighty-pounds of damsons" (the nearby Lyth Valley is famous for them). The pub's bartering currency is free puddings: "Our damson crème brulée is something else."

Emma still works in the kitchen but has a head chef, Richard Price, to share the workload and ideas. Everything, bar the ice cream (which comes from Kendal) is made on the premises, and to order. "We have a freezer but it only holds bread, ice cream and emergency soup."

The food that draws people here includes ribeye steak with herby-stuffed tomato, roasted belly of pork with haricot beans and smoked sausage, scallops in puff pastry with organic watercress sauce. They have burgers on the menu but theirs are sandwiched in a homemade bun with homemade coleslaw and chutney. Tagines and curries are popular, too.

"Our plates look lovely but there's no fussiness," she adds. "Our puddings are not fancy but fabulous."

There are no hovering waiters but Lesley, the front-of-house manager, has a sixth sense and seems to know when you want something and barman Mike greets you with a cheery wave. They have been with Emma a long time and many of the young waiting staff worked here while at school and return in university holidays.

The pub is a community centre, too. On Wednesdays, Emma runs a Community Lunch that is two courses for £5 and people share a table and cement friendships. "When our Post Office closed last year, there was nowhere else that could act as a meeting place," she says. "The lunch is for anyone and the only proviso is that everyone sits together!" A no-choice menu keeps the costs down and spirits are always high. The pub is popular for charity events, reunions, wedding anniversaries and family celebrations. It's stolen the heart of the community in a way that's taken Emma by surprise. "Some people come every week – and they like to sit in 'their' chair. I'm happy that they feel so at home."

The Lunesdale Arms

Evening main courses £9–£15.95
Best meal deal: ask about mid-week offers
No food on Monday
Nearest train: Wennington

Low Sizergh Farm

Sizergh Kendal
Cumbria LA8 8AE
015395 60426 www.lowsizerghbarn.co.uk

Low Sizergh Barn is much more than a grocery store, it plays a crucial part in Cumbria's food economy and community. "My parents, who opened the shop in 1991, soon realised they were part of a fragile network of small, rural businesses that relied on the actions of each other for survival," says Alison Park. "Previously producers supplied directly through town markets, and now farm shops can continue that tradition. We take what's in season and specific to this region. That diversity across the country makes every region special, and is part of our culture."

Inside the Westmorland stone barn – beautifully renovated and late seventeenth century – are homemade cakes, jams, chutneys, cheeses, pies, meats and arts and crafts, with a buzzing café above. Alison also sells organic eggs from their own hens (which outshone supermarket free-range by miles in Rick Stein's taste test), organic vegetables from Growing Well, the social enterprise based on the farm, and organic milk, cheese and ice cream from her brother Richard's dairy herd. And you will find some of the friendliest staff.

Low Sizergh Farm – 'Sizergh' is Norse for summer pasture – was conventionally farmed by Richard's family for years. In 2000 the whole family decided to go organic: "It was daunting," recalls Richard "for farming organically challenges you as a farmer and requires more of your knowledge and skill." Richard crossed his Holstein Friesians, which is a breed suited to intensive systems, with Swedish Reds and Montbéliardes. He let cows come into heat naturally rather than using hormones and put them on 'clean' fields not recently grazed, to avoid the need for chemical worming treatments.

Organic milk comes from cows not exposed to pesticides, fed on GMOs or routinely given antibiotics. The organic cows' diet of clovers and grasses, with only limited cereals and concentrates, results in milk higher in omega-3 fatty acids, vitamin E and beta-carotene (vitamin A); skimmed milk devotees beware – these nutrients reside in the fat.

"We always knew organic milk was very different and better and to have the health benefits scientifically proven is helpful," says Richard.

"Milk is a delicate product and its quality is maintained by handling it as little as possible. We transport ours just eight miles to be bottled."

The milk finds its way into third generation Lancashire cheese-maker Chris Sandham's 'Kendal Creamy' and 'Kendal Crumbly' cheeses and into Steve Duffin's Windermere ice creams.

Up a grassy path from the farm shop lie growing plots and polytunnels tended by workers from Growing Well. The social enterprise brings together a group of volunteers, all of whom are recovering from mental health issues. They cultivate vegetables to sell through the shop and elsewhere and get involved in promotion of their produce and all aspects of running the organisation.

"There's nothing quite like feeling the warmth of the soil and seeing things grow"

KING OF THE PIPPINS

Their horticultural endeavours result in increased self-confidence, crucial for returning to the world of work.

"Our alliance is perfect: we wanted excellent produce for the shop and Growing Well needed land for their project. There's nothing quite like feeling the warmth of the soil and seeing things grow," says Richard, who has been inspired to resume vegetable growing himself.

Growing Well also hosts educational visits, NVQ horticulture courses and one-day workshops on such subjects as compost-making, apple grafting and seed sowing. "We're planning a CSA (Community Supported Agriculture) whereby people will buy a share of the crop," says Alison, who sits on the board. "I love that philosophy of people investing time, money and commitment, and wish it was more widespread in agriculture." Richard enjoys having so many people about, "like farms were before machinery replaced labour."

Traditional apples have been planted, including Keswick Codlin, Greenup's Pippin and Bloody Ploughman (said to be reddened by the blood of a scrumping peasant slain by a ruthless landowner). A local group is testing which varieties are commercially viable. The Parks are also helping revive the Westmorland damson, a local species protected by Slow Food's 'Ark of Taste'. The damson was threatened with extinction after the local wool industry – that used great quantities of them for wool dyes – went into decline. You'll find the Westmorland in jam, chutney, beer, gin and ice cream at the Barn.

The café is hugely popular with locals and holidaymakers. Between 1.15 and 3.30, maybe over a slice of the spiced Cumberland tart Rum Nicky (created in the days when the northwest's ports traded in exotic dried fruits and spices), you'll see the cows being milked in the parlour. Then take a wander among the nutritious clover fields on the farm trail.

"It's been fabulous to see how people respond – they discover what goes into milk, how we manage the land, rear calves, feed them and give them shelter. People are amazed that the production of milk is so complex."

Gilpin Lodge

Crook Road Windermere
Cumbria LA23 3NE
015394 88818 www.gilpinlodge.co.uk

"Tourism and farming must work hand in hand," says Barney Cunliffe. "We source from small farms, helping them stay afloat and look after the countryside which draws the tourists. The footpaths, stone walls and woodlands those farmers maintain are essential for the Lake District."

Gilpin Lodge hides down a lane, enclosed by woodland and craggy moorland. Owned by the Cunliffe family since 1917, it has been a family-run hotel since 1987. "Mum specialises in interiors, dad and I are on the business and marketing side, my wife on guests and my brother is our architect." In the last decade Barney has seen a sea change in local agriculture. "People have realised their small, hilly farms can't compete with huge industrial ones, so they're diversifying. Now I can get rare breed pork and beef, dairy products and even salt marsh grazed rose veal."

Middle White pork from Savin Hill Farm ranges free in the beautiful Lyth Valley. Hams come from Richard Woodall in nearby Waberthwaite, an eighth-generation family business renowned for its traditional curing.

Native Cumbrian beef is supplied by Andrew Sharp, a passionate mutton advocate who runs butchery classes locally and at London's Borough Market. And Cream of Cumbria near Carlisle provides very special butter. Within two days of milking, double cream from local herds is churned, washed and shaped by hand. "It's extremely fresh and lasts only two weeks as there are no additives."

Shaggy Herdwick sheep have been bred here for centuries. They stick to particular fells, giving farmers no need for fences. "Hazel Relph at Yew Tree Farm lets them graze a full year, so they have a deeper flavour, enhanced by the heathers and herbs they eat. She takes them to slaughter to keep them calm. I hate seeing animals hurtling along the motorway scared out of their minds."

Chef Russell Plowman will drag Barney into the kitchen to admire a beautiful fish, lobster or joint of meat, almost too in awe to weald his knife. "His roast Herdwick loin is delicious served with rich jus and vegetables picked that morning," says Barney. When Hazel from Yew Tree took a well-earned holiday Russell instantly knew, as the meat was less tender and they presumed Hazel's stand-in didn't have quite such a soothing touch.

Russell pairs classic flavours: Jerusalem artichoke velouté with truffle oil; dived scallops with cauliflower purée and smoked bacon; Stichelton cheese soufflé with Waldorf salad (see page 144); gnocchi with squash and sage; rice pudding with prunes and Armagnac. Everything is made from scratch, from homemade biscuits at elevenses to petits fours after dinner.

Russell's larder is capacious: grouse, pheasant, hare and venison from surrounding woodlands; prawns, cockles and bass from Morecombe Bay; dived scallops and langoustines from Scotland; and an abundance of vegetables from neighbouring Lancashire. There are acres of garden, but Barney is cautious about growing their own. "I wouldn't want a token gesture. So many places make a song and dance about their kitchen garden, but in reality they're buying in the majority, especially in winter."

Reed beds process waste laundry water, solar panels help heat staff accommodation, and insulation for new buildings is well above the norm. A woodchip boiler is next. "I need to be in control, so we're stock-piling wood and planting more trees. At a hotel you can't say, 'sorry, there's not enough wind or light today!'"

Gilpin Lodge

Set five-course dinner menu £52.50
Best meal deal: Mon-Sat 3-course lunch £25
Afternoon tea £16.50 3.30-5.30
Nearest train: Oxenholme

"We source from small farms, helping them stay afloat and look after the countryside which draws the tourists"

Slack House Farm

Gilsland Brampton
Cumbria CA8 7DB 016977 47351
www.slackhousefarm.co.uk

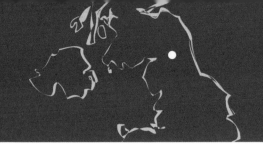

Bread and cheese make perfect partners, unless they are being made in the same kitchen. Eric Horn's first kitchen-made cheeses were colonised by yeasts from wife Dianne's bread-making making them explode. Thirty years later, having moved their pedigree Ayrshire dairy herd from West Yorkshire to Cumbria and, having achieved organic status, Eric's raw milk Birdoswald cheese is creating a big stir in the markets, farmshops and restaurants of northern England. He and Dianne are proud to join the fight to save Britain's farmhouse cheeses.

The recipe for Ayrshire wholemilk, hard cheese was brought from Ireland to Scotland in 1688. Initially, the warm milk from the evening's milking was left in a vat to naturally sour overnight. Today, food standards require a culture of known organisms to be used to sour the milk before a vegetable rennet is added to set it. The process involves 'cheddaring', not unique to Cheddar, whereby bricks of drained curds are repeatedly stacked and turned in a warm vat. Following milling, salting and pressing, the cheese is bandaged in cloth and ripened for up to six months. The result is a creamy yet crumbly, mellow cheese with a lovely lingering aftertaste.

Slack House Farm's organic beef and lamb is available through Hadrian Organics, a small group of farms who share market stalls, farm equipment and surplus crops.

The Horns are also involved in making the Hadrian's Wall corridor, from Carlisle to Newcastle, the first fairtrade World Heritage site. "All fairtrade tea and coffee plantations are cooperatives, owned by the people who work them. Worldwide, more people work in cooperatives than multinationals. Isn't that cheering?" asks Dianne, who cites the increasing number of social enterprises as one positive outcome of the credit crunch.

The Horns converted the old cowshed into a visitor centre, tearoom and farmshop. The Scypen ('cowshed' in old English) is run as a social enterprise with several other women and open for lunch and tea, serving only local produce and homemade food. Evening meals can be booked in advance. Dianne refuses to be just an 'organic where possible' cook. Roman flavours infuse the menu, inspired by the local cuisine of two millennia past: venison rissoles come paired with redcurrant and wine sauce and flavoured with coriander, a spice loved by ancient Romans; cabbage comes Roman-style, with leeks, olive oil and caraway. "And," says Dianne, "did you know the Romans invented haggis?"

Around the tearoom, notices alert customers to the use of unpasteurised milk. The Horns wouldn't dream of using anything else.

"Ordinary milk has been standardised, homogenised and pasteurised – even the organic milk." says Dianne. "The enzymes and the proteins have been denatured. The enzyme lactase, which is needed to digest lactose milk sugar, is one of those. This could be a contributing factor in lactose intolerance."

In 2007 Eric's milk, which is just filtered and cooled, nothing more, won an award for being the cleanest consistently in the region. Next door Eric makes his Birdoswald cheese twice a week, with a crowd of curious faces peering through the viewing window to admire his craft.

Dianne is on a mission to reconnect people with agriculture. "People have become divorced from the production of real food. Supermarkets sell industrial food that's so processed I don't consider it to be food." Dianne designs children's activities to track milk from soil to bottle. "We look at soil microbes, clover root nodules, the diversity of the grassland, cows grazing and the milking

parlours." She also shows the children how to make Roman spelt bread.

An abundance of views surround Slack House Farm's one-hundred-and-twelve acres of open countryside, with the Pennines and North Lakes to the South and Hadrian's Wall disappearing off to the East and West. 'Tip' the elderly border collie earns her keep by gathering the cows and Dorset Mule sheep, if somewhat more slowly than in her youth. She now has an apprentice, Bess.

As part of the Countryside Stewardship Scheme, the Horns maintain drystone walls, hedgerows, woodlands and waterways – all vital wildlife habitats. They may look dry, but the stone walls harbour weasels, rabbits, voles and mice, with wrens and pied wagtails choosing them for nesting sites.

The Feathers Inn

Hedley on the Hill Stocksfield
Northumberland NE43 7SW
01661 843607 www.thefeathers.net

"We're the meeting place for pretty much everything in the village," muses Helen Greer. "There's the Leek Club, Parish Council meetings, farmers' market, fund-raising events, beer festival, minibus pick-up point and we're the polling station... The Feathers is a true 'local', a bringer-together of people."

With its sweeping views north to Hadrian's Wall – and, on a good day, over Newcastle to the coast – the 200-year-old inn also serves award-winning, classic pub and traditional north-eastern dishes. Neither a gastropub nor a pub with a restaurant tagged on, it's a place where diners sit among drinkers, traditional beams, swirly carpets and whisky jugs, and where the only clues that the food might be exceptional are the shelves of well-thumbed cookery books, the knowledgeable young staff and the air of unhurried contentment.

pan haggerty (fried potatoes, onion and cheese).

"Local food needs local produce," says Helen, "and, for us, local sourcing addresses environmental issues." Apart from lemons, oils and spices, all their produce comes from the region. Their beef and sheep supplies can often be seen from the pub as they graze the surrounding pastures; their rare breed pork is from across the river Tyne. Fish is landed at North Shields and Sunderland, or hooked from nearby rivers; game is shot on local estates; rare varieties of potatoes are grown in the Scottish borders; farmhouse cheeses are from makers in Northumberland and Teesdale.

Helen and Rhian grow many of their herbs, and forage for wild sorrel and garlic. They stock locally brewed ales, fruit and berry cordials and soft drinks, and their fairtrade coffees are roasted and ground here in Northumberland,

Helen and husband and chef Rhian Cradock bought the pub in 2007. Brought up in County Durham in a food-loving family, Rhian learnt on the job, working in restaurants in Liverpool while a student, followed by London, including a spell at the Michelin-starred Chez Bruce in Wandsworth. Wanting to run his own show and to create a place that offered well-cooked, honest and affordable dishes – a food, rather than a foodie, destination – Rhian decided to return to his native North East. It also meant he could recreate one of his great-aunts' tasty, but largely forgotten, dishes such as ham and pease pudding and

then mixed to create The Feathers' own house blend.

Commercial supplies are supplemented by a healthy bartering trade with customers: perhaps pigeons and rabbits from a weekend shoot or bags of surplus beetroot, lettuces and chanterelle mushrooms. "Villagers never tell us where they get the mushrooms from," says Helen, "their foraging spots are closely guarded secrets and they are usually paid in pints of beer."

The daily-changing menus are at the mercy of their suppliers. After a flurry of morning calls – perhaps a large turbot has been landed or a farmer has some unsold pork belly – Rhian makes his menu decisions. "The lunchtime

Please feel free to browse our selection of books.....

menu is conjured up just before we open and is usually warm off the printer for the first customers," says Helen.

When asked what they don't make, Helen comes up with three items: smoked salmon, Cumberland sausage ("we make our ordinary sausages") and ice cream. "We haven't the space and Wheelbirks, the farm at the bottom of the hill, makes such good ice cream from their Jersey cows it seems silly to compete." Everything else, from breads to yogurts, pâtés to preserves is made in their kitchen.

"We often buy a whole animal and do the butchery ourselves," she explains. "We get to use more of the animal and it helps the farmers and keeps prices down." So, you might find sweetbreads or black pudding on the menu as well as home-made corned beef, rabbit or pigeon pie. Fish and chips is a staple, often using ling

away. And there are very limited services for recycling other materials, such as paper and cardboard."

Helen and Rhian are passionate about reducing their environmental footprint: checking seals on fridges and freezers, using pot plants instead of cut flowers (because of transport costs and pesticide use) and using rainwater for their garden.

Intelligent customer service is another of Helen's hobby-horses. "It's not all about food; it's about the whole experience. With staff, we try to instil a pride in where they work. If they have a good rapport with diners they will go away happier and the staff will enjoy their job more." Staff are given a dining discount so they can bring their family for a meal, relax and experience what dining here is all about.

The old-fashioned hearty menu makes their business

or coley rather than the endangered Atlantic cod; Rhian's burnt Northumbrian cream has a loyal following. Rhian produces imaginative vegetarian dishes, too - the sort of thing that most people wouldn't cook at home.

The pub's demand has encouraged local producers to diversify. One farmer now rears geese and turkey while the ice cream producer, with Rhian's help, has created a range of sorbets using another farmer's glut of apples.

Helen wishes the local council was equally responsive when it comes to recycling services. "We recycle our glass but have to pay for them to take it

work. Says Helen: "It's about getting the best produce and keeping costs down while supporting local farmers who are also our regulars."

The Feathers Inn

Evening main courses £9–£20
Wine club events organised
No food Sunday evening or all day Monday
Nearest train: Stocksfield

173

Wales

Key

Alastair Sawday's Special Places to eat
Soil Association certified organic producers

Map 6

Wales

Gliffaes Hotel

Gliffaes Road Crickhowell
Powys NP8 1RH
01874 730371 www.gliffaeshotel.com

"Being green is more expensive and creates more work, but we can't keep throwing things into landfill and wasting resources. We live in one of the most stunning locations in Wales, in the heart of the Brecon Beacons National Park, surrounded by enormous biodiversity. We want to pass it on to our children the way we found it."

James Suter and his wife Susie are third generation custodians of Gliffaes Hotel, a grand Victorian house with jaw-dropping views to the river Usk and the Black Mountains. City escapees sink into beds, books and baths, the active ride the tandem to biking trails, anglers head off to the river to catch brown trout for the chef to cook. "Many of them came as children in Susie's grandparents' day and we love welcoming them back with their children," says James.

There are giant Californian sequoias and other rare and magnificent specimens in the formal gardens; scrub and fallen trees are left untouched, artificial sprays never used, beehives kept to pollinate wild flowers. The result is a haven for wildlife: kingfishers, dippers, buzzards and red kites visit and there's a tremendous dawn chorus and clouds of returning house martins, swallows and swifts. At night tawny owls hoot, hedgehogs scurry and ten species of bat emerge from the attic.

Living in such a magical spot, the Suters felt compelled to 'go green'. As well as the usual recycling, they use an accelerated composter to save a tonne of food waste from landfill each month and to fertilise the

vegetable patch; their own spring water replaces bottled; roof and curtains are insulated with sheep's wool; washing is dried al fresco; log fires fuelled by their own sustainably managed woods heat several rooms.

James and Susie support the Slow Food movement, particularly its emphasis on using local producers. "I'd rather buy from farmers here than insist on using particular rare breeds or organic alternatives from further afield. We're surrounded by traditional hill farms that produce excellent meat." Beef and lamb come from nearby Middlewood Farm, free-range chicken from Llandinam, game from the Suters' own shoots and smoked fish from Black Mountains Smokery.

"Local fruit and vegetables are more elusive," says James. "I asked for Pembrokeshire potatoes and the box arrived with 'Egypt' on the label." One trusted source is Penpont Estate's organic walled garden in Brecon, and of course the hotel's own patch and orchard. James and Susie forage, too.

The Welsh cheeseboard includes the sheep's milk cheese Caws Mynydd Du ('Black Mountains cheese'), made a few peaks away, brie-style Perl Wen ('white pearl') and hard Perl Las ('blue pearl'), made near Cardigan from organic milk.

Chef Karl Cheetham, who trained here years ago and vowed to return, runs a happy kitchen. His passion is butchery and of course he uses every bit of meat to produce brawn and ham hock terrines, roasted racks and slow-braised shanks. "British food improves each year and I encourage our cooks to eat and work elsewhere to learn," says James.

The Suters and Karl meet weekly to discuss what's in season and to set daily menus. "I'd rather not offer choice," says James. "We'd waste less, and it would be cheaper for customers too. At a friend's dinner party you wouldn't ask for an alternative to what they are offering, would you? But customers' diverse tastes and allergies make that unrealistic."

Teatime is a grand occasion. Walkers and fishermen flock for dainty sandwiches, warm scones, Karl's bara brith (speckled bread), sweetened with spices and dried fruit, and griddled Welsh cakes. Kate Gladwyn supplies a Land Rover-full of her home-made cakes each week.

Wood panelling, contemporary Welsh art and wood-burning stove provide the cosy winter setting for dinner. In summer, in the conservatory and on the terrace you bask in sunshine and views. "People change for dinner out of respect for the food and cooking," explains James, "but there's a relaxed atmosphere and it's usually only me that's wearing a tie!"

Food is Modern British through a Mediterranean lens: duck liver parfait with homemade brioche and caramelised onions; smoked venison and fig terrine with blueberry compote; goat's cheese and watercress ravioli; rack of Welsh lamb with redcurrant jus; pear pithivier with chilli and rosemary ice cream.

James is passionate about using sustainable fish. Cod and tuna have left the menu and the rest is Marine Stewardship Council approved: lemon sole with beurre blanc and new potatoes; whole roast line-caught sea bass; seared dived scallops with crispy pancetta; pan-fried bream with mussel and saffron chowder. "It limits choice, but we cannot continue raping the seas. If people could see the state of affairs beneath the surface, they'd agree."

Gliffaes Hotel

Evening main courses £12–£22
Best meal deal: Thursday 2–course lunch £10
Meals always available. Closed January
Nearest train: Abergavenny

The Felin Fach Griffin

Felin Fach Brecon
Powys LD3 0UB 01874 620111
www.felinfachgriffin.co.uk

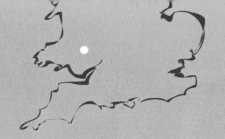

A stock pot burbles on the Aga while guests start the day with eggs from the hens, homemade sausages and homemade bread toasted and spread with Welsh butter and kitchen garden jams. This could be a scene from the Inkin brothers' childhood growing up on a farm in Monmouthshire, where their mother grew vegetables and cooked everything from scratch.

"We were incredibly lucky and try to maintain those values here," says Edmund Inkin who looks after this pub, near Brecon, while brother Charles runs their second pub, the Gurnard's Head in Cornwall (see page 20). "I'd been a banker in London. In hindsight that was so unreal; here I can see the real difference we make for customers, staff and suppliers. And it's heaps more fun."

The Black Mountains and the Felin Fach Griffin draw energetic holiday-makers, literary folk descend during the Hay Festival, and food-lovers all year round. The Griffin is known for its superb food: goats' curd with roasted bell pepper, black olives and basil, line-caught bass with cauliflower and truffle shavings, caramel poached pineapple with passion fruit sorbet and coriander jus.

Julie Bell who hosts here has an infectious Irish cheer and her style has attracted regulars. "We reserve tables for drinkers, rotate local bitters and stouts to keep all factions happy, and hold beer and wine tastings. We've introduced set menus at lower prices, and edged the cooking back down to earth."

Unusually for a pub, given the paperwork and expense involved, the kitchen garden is certified organic. "That approach attracted me here," says Julie, who grew up not believing friends who said that carrots came in bags, or peas from the freezer. "It's had positive repercussions throughout the business."

Gardener Joe Hand works closely with chef Simon Potter to plan crops of beans, spinach, artichokes, leeks, cabbages, broccoli and soft fruits. In spring, peas and broad beans are picked and shelled just hours before being stirred into risotto with fresh mint. At summer's end, pickled gherkins and green tomato chutney are hoarded for a year of ploughman's lunches.

Chefs fuse classical French training with local ingredients: home-cured salmon with celeriac remoulade and toasted sourdough, homemade venison sausages with cassoulet and bruschette; gnocchi with butternut squash and wild mushrooms; Welsh cakes with crème Anglaise spiked with Penderyn Welsh whisky.

Good quality meat is available in abundance: pork is supplied by two nearby farmers, beef and lamb come from a traditional butcher in Brecon, venison from a farm near Bwlch and pheasant from local shoots. The Wye valley is renowned for asparagus, and Welsh farmhouse cheeses enhance the all-British cheeseboard, including sheep's milk Caws Mynydd Du and flavourful Gorwydd Caerphilly.

The charcuterie plate features house-cured meats and salamis from Trealy Farm near Monmouth. "They use traditional breeds, farmed in a sustainable way, and have spent many years researching traditional curing methods," says Edmund.

Other speciality ingredients travel further: Turkish figs, Italian truffles and spuds from Carroll's Heritage Potatoes in Northumberland. They use Red Duke of York potatoes for fluffy gnocchi, Yukon Golds for buttery yellow mash, bright white Sharpe's Express and Witchhills for boiling – each is a reminder that thousands more varieties of this humble Andean tuber exist than the handful available in supermarkets.

"The starting point should be the skill and creativity of your team, not some 'gastropub' menu template," says Edmund, who encourages cooks to eat in top restaurants and visit producers for inspiration. Meanwhile Julie involves all staff in tastings and food pairing trials for her drinks list. (Try venison stew with Wye Valley Brewery's Dorothy Goodbody Wholesome stout.) And twice a year Edmund and Julie treat staff to their own cooking and an afternoon of rounders. The aim is to promote from within, and it works.

"More locals are coming," says Edmund. "The schoolmaster who drops in on his way home, the local MP, the regulars who meet at table thirteen every Thursday night. "It's quite an achievement for an area which has largely lost its pub tradition. With no post office or village shop and the church not playing the role it once did, we're hoping the Griffin can become the fulcrum of Felin Fach and the surrounding parishes."

The Felin Fach Griffin

Evening main courses £14.50–£18.50
Best meal deal: 3-course set supper, £26.50
Food always available
Nearest train: Abergavenny

Elan Valley Mutton

Henfron Elan Valley Rhayader
Powys LD6 5HE 01597 811240
www.elanvalleymutton.co.uk

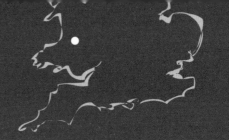

If Tony Davies' great-great-grandfather could see Henfron Farm now, he would hardly notice the difference. Here in the remote Elan Valley, in mid-Wales, seventeen-hundred acres of wind- and rain-swept moorland, peat bogs and heathered hillsides sustain the Davies' resilient Welsh Mountain sheep, just as they have for centuries.

"The role of farmer is two-fold: producing food and looking after the countryside for future generations.

There may be global food shortage scares, but we mustn't go mad producing it, leaving nothing for tomorrow. Our sheep keep bracken and brambles under control, while we maintain hedgerows, woodlands and ponds and, thereby, wildlife," says Angela Davies.

As fifth generation custodians of Henfron ('old hillside'), Tony and Angela were determined the farm would not falter on their watch. Keen to engage with the public and sell direct, they forged relationships with the

local slaughterhouse and butcher and took the bold step of switching to mutton, which is killed after several years.

"We'd always eaten mutton, and friends and family raved about our roasts. Keeping wethers, castrated males, has long been practised here, with the mutton sold to locals. Flocks are 'hefted': born and bred on the same mountain for generations. But without wethers on the uplands year-round, the next farm's flocks will stray onto the lengthening grass."

The Davies allow their sheep to reach three or four years old. Only the odd 'ugly' lamb meets an early end, since any defects will compromise its ability to survive. Kept lean through exercise, ewes bear only one lamb, so are better able to protect them from foxes and crows. The sheep spend their lives on the hillsides, only receiving organic bought-in feed in particularly harsh years. With such a healthy lifestyle, it's no wonder disease is rare.

Tony checks his flocks on horseback. "Other farmers use quad-bikes, but our men love their horses, that keep them warm, know every crease of the hillside and offer a better vantage point. On a foggy afternoon they make it back in time for tea while the quad-bikers are still going in circles," says Angela.

Mutton was once one of Britain's most loved meats. "Saddle of mutton is a joint for an epicure," wrote Dorothy Hartley, a food historian, in 1954. But around this time factors converged to start its decline: imported New Zealand lamb; working women with less time for slow-cooking; post-war affluence expanding the privilege of eating immature animals and expensive cuts.

Recently a niche market for the rich meat has appeared. "At first we hunted out foodies at food festivals who were always game for trying new things. Now people find us, having seen celebrity chefs using mutton,"

says Angela, who is an active member of the Mutton Renaissance campaign. "Not all mutton is equal. The best is from traditional slow-growing breeds, and hung for two weeks to tenderise. Our mutton is deep red, marbled but not fatty, and tasty because of our herb-rich meadows."

Angela loves a meltingly tender slow-roasted leg joint, Tony is partial to curry made from shoulder meat, and their children opt for leg steaks, burgers and noisette cutlets. The family favourite is cawl, a Welsh stew of mutton neck, bacon and root vegetables, once cooked in every farmhouse in large cauldrons suspended over fires. The various cuts are sold by mail-order and at independent stores in Wales. Angela provides recipes including a Moroccan tagine and an Elizabethan stew spiced with cinnamon, ginger, cloves and mace.

A visit to Rome resulted in a popular mutton and rosemary salami, and a spicy chorizo-style sausage.

"We've had to re-educate people about mutton. But whenever they try it, they love it," says Angela. "We're both foodies, so it doesn't feel like work."

"I used to grow tomatoes for supermarkets but then they rejected them because they weren't the right shape," says Anne Segger. "The buyer that visited had to admit they tasted wonderful but said he couldn't take them. Taste is something that so often gets forgotten in the pursuit of uniform appearance and predictable cropping."

Anne and partner Peter Segger were organic pioneers and arrived here in the seventies determined to prove vegetables could be grown without artificial sprays. They helped stimulate public demand by supplying supermarkets with an organic version of popular vegetables, but now they leave the main crops to larger farms while they concentrate on increasing the varieties of vegetables they grow – everything from artichokes to aubergines. Almost everything produced on Blaencamel Farm, near pretty Aberaeron on Cardigan Bay, is sold locally, too.

Unlike most new farmers, they stuck it out and indeed became instrumental in making organic food a mainstream possibility. Peter formed Organic Farm Foods to supply supermarkets with Welsh organic produce. "It was hugely significant, the commercial equivalent of the Soil Association's campaigns," says Anne, who meanwhile took the helm at Blaencamel. "At first, other farmers thought we were crazy to try to grow organically. Now they marvel at the vegetables we produce from the incredibly stony soil in this glacial valley."

In unheated greenhouses and fields over fifty vegetables grow, along with salad leaves, herbs and fruits. The produce is sold at the small farm gate shop, through son Tom's box scheme in Cardiff, farmers' markets, restaurants and shops. Blaencamel only sells its own produce since there are at least ten items available at any time: spring greens from January, early potatoes, wet garlic and radishes from March, mixed herbs and salad leaves all year. To help fill the 'hungry gap', when most farms have scant offerings, there are always winter root vegetables and also preserves made from previous gluts such as pickled beetroot and tomato passata.

Anne alerts local chefs to new produce and they come to raid her market stall. "It's very flattering," she says. Her heirloom tomatoes – pink Brandywines, stripy Tigerellas, San Marzano plums – make wonderful mixed platters. "Our produce has such intense flavours and people have noticed improvements over time, which must reflect what's happening in the soil." Anne grows some 'open pollinated' varieties in place of laboratory-selected F1-hybrids. "They can crop less predictably but are often more flavoursome."

Peter has a compost 'recipe' that he learnt in South Africa and South America. Called 'Controlled Microbial Composting', the system uses specific ratios of nitrogen and carbon-rich materials, manure and clay, combined with eagle-eyed temperature and carbon dioxide monitoring, to create a fertiliser which counteracts soil disease.

"There are billions of micro-organisms, and each has a job. Spreading this compost inoculates the soil. As in wild yeast 'starters' for bread, the beneficial micro-organisms out-colonise the pathogens," explains Anne. Such a start in life can even mitigate against mould on fruit after harvest. "I don't understand why more farmers don't use this system. People tend to be very proud of their own composting systems and resistant to change."

Peter meticulously totted up greenhouse gas emissions, including customers' car journeys and methane from the sheep, then subtracted carbon captured through their untouched meadows, ancient woodland and hedgerows. The result was astounding: each year Blaencamel captures more than it emits, mainly due to their ban on artificial

fertilisers and the carbon sequestered by their composting.

"Thirty per cent of the UK's greenhouse gases come from farming and food. If every farm did as we do, we would reduce emissions by two hundred million tonnes and would be well on the way to being carbon neutral," says Peter, who has tirelessly promoted Transition Towns in Wales, a movement for sustainable living in the face of peak oil and climate change.

"We love having people on the farm," says Anne, who gets schoolchildren daring each other to try rocket and coriander. "We host numerous gardeners, farmers and researchers keen to unravel Blaencamel's horticultural secrets. Footpaths criss-criss all over. One Christmas Peter presented me with an album of two-hundred flowers he'd discovered here! In spring the carpets of wild daffodils in the woods are beyond belief and before that come snowdrops, wood anemones, wood sorrel, bluebells and marsh marigolds."

Whenever you come, pop into the shop; it's open twenty-four hours a day, every day, with an honesty box. "There's always something there freshly picked that morning," says Anne.

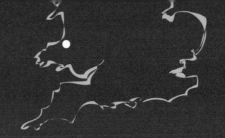

Holden Farm Dairy

Bwlchwernen Fawr Llangybi Lampeter
Ceredigion SA48 8PS
01570 493283 www.hafodcheese.co.uk

"Our cheese is definitely 'slow'. It comes from a slower, more sustainable way of farming and reflects the land and people that made it, rather than being a product of machines." Rachel and Sam Holden's beautifully golden Hafod (pronounced 'havod') ranks alongside Britain's finest cheddars.

The small dairy is deep in rural West Wales on Bwlchwernen Farm, that is owned by Sam's father Patrick Holden, Director of the Soil Association. It is the longest established organic dairy farm in Wales and Patrick has developed the organic standards for dairy farming here since 1973. Although mostly consumed by his involvement in the Soil Association, Patrick still milks his sixty-five blotchy brown and white cows at weekends. To build resilience in the face of rising fossil fuel costs, he grows the vast majority of the cows' feed here, rather than importing it.

Sam and Rachel had quit their London office jobs when Patrick suggested they make cheese. He had been inspired by two pioneers: the late Dougal Campbell, who had used Patrick's milk to make T'yn Grug cheese and trained many others, and Randolph Hodgson, a leading light in Britain's cheese renaissance.

"We were trained by Simon Jones, who makes Lincolnshire Poacher, and Joe Schneider (also in this book), who makes Stichelton. The whole cheese-making community welcomed us with open arms," recall Rachel and Sam, who invested two years, a government grant and bank loan into building the dairy.

Hafod's recipe is based on Lincolnshire Poacher, itself developed from T'yn Grug. It stands out for being organic and unpasteurised, and made from Ayrshire milk. "Ayrshires aren't popular, because they have low yields, but their milk is wonderfully rich in butterfat and protein. Other cheddars turn pale in winter, when cows are indoors eating silage, but Hafod stays deep gold," says Rachel, who sells the cheese by mail-order, onsite and through cheesemongers.

Every other day, seventeen-hundred litres of milk is heated in the Dutch vat and set with rennet. At just the right moment, Sam cuts the soft jelly and it separates into curds and whey. The curds are cooked and drained, reducing to ten per cent of the original milk's volume. It is then 'cheddared' – cut into slabs and stacked up – and transforms from scrambled egg to cooked chicken breast texture. Finally it is milled, salted and moulded. "The process takes so long that soft cheese makers think cheddar makers are crazy," says Rachel.

Proof of a successful day's cheese-making is not confirmed for at least a year. During this time the cheese lose moisture and develop a firm texture and rich buttery, nutty flavour with a slight tang. Near the rind, where moulds are most active, it becomes almost Parmesan-like.

"Block cheese manufacturers aim to retain moisture to maintain weight, hence the vacuum-packing. Its flavour is standardised, whereas ours reflects our cows' natural diet, different as they move during the year. We can afford not to pasteurise as we have total control over our herd and milking; that's almost impossible if you're sourcing milk from hundreds of farms. Raw milk cheese retains more complex flavours. Sometimes you can taste the meadow flowers and the flavours of our slow-growing grass."

While male calves are a waste product of dairy farming, under organic certification they are protected from being sold to continental-style veal systems. "People don't realise how intensive most of the industry is. If you care about animal welfare, you should buy organic," insists Rachel.

Farmhouse cheese-making is still only a drop in the cheese ocean so the Holdens unite with fellow artisans to promote their cheese at festivals and farmers markets. "The Slow Food movement has really helped," says Rachel. "At their huge 'Cheese' event in Italy, it was incredibly motivating to see so many like-minded cheese-makers from all over the world. Together we have power."

"*The process takes so long that soft cheese makers think cheddar makers are crazy*"

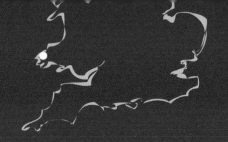

Caerfai Farm
St David's Pembrokeshire SA62 6QT
01437 720548
www.cawscaerfai.co.uk

Wyn Evans remembers the time St David's, out on Wales's windswept westernmost tip, was isolated by a severe blizzard. "The only milk that reached our city was mine. People queued with jugs." On a normal day, when rivers of ordinary milk are transported to dairy processors across Britain, Wyn struggles to sell his organic milk.

"It's ironic: everyone's talking about food security yet I'm being paid to produce less milk." When Wyn started farming there were thirty-five dairy farms in the parish. Now there are three. He has watched hundreds of acres cease producing food. "It will take massive investment to make that land productive again."

Supermarket sales of organic dairy products have

food security, they'll have to pay a proper price for decent, local food. Did you know, if the M25 closed for six hours all supermarkets in the area would run out of milk?"

In 1977 he acquired a small 'biodigester' to extract methane from the slurry of two cows. His current "seventy-cow" upgrade has churned away happily for thirty years, fuelling farmhouse Aga and dairy. "I feed the biodigester with campers' sewage, whey from cheese-making and slurry from the cows. Forty per cent of energy consumed by a cow comes out as methane, so by putting cow slurry into the digester, heating it and adding other waste, I can capture the gases for renewable energy. I'm trying to close the energy loops," says Wyn.

When digested slurry is put on the land it removes far

fallen during the economic downturn ("they've cleared shelves to make space for 'value' items"), so most of Wyn's organic milk is sold as conventional and he has been advised to cut production. "Supermarkets go to the end of the world, literally, to get cheap food. But when climate change and peak oil come into the equation, they won't be able to. We'll need local food. If people want long-term

less oxygen compared with undigested slurry. When soil lacks oxygen earthworms rise to the surface where they are picked off by birds; wormless soil is less fertile and prone to flash-flooding.

Media focus on climate change around the millennium fired Wyn's commitment to further reduce his footprint. There are now several ground-source heat-

Caerfai organic

pumps, eight solar thermal systems, photo-voltaic panels and a wind turbine installed on the farm. "In my grandchildren's lifetimes there will be huge problems. I don't want their children asking why I didn't do anything."

The severe droughts of 1976 and 1984 prompted the switch to organic farming: Wyn noticed fields on which he'd used soluble nitrogen fertiliser were worst hit, whereas old leas of permanent pasture fared best. "If you feed grass from above, its roots have no need to dig deep, so in a drought it dies." Wyn also found the varied grasses were better for cows' health. "If you ate the same thing every day, you'd be deficient in nutrients, too." The deep roots in the permanent pastures pull up trace elements, too, which are good for the cows' immune systems.

But Wyn would be even less likely to homogenise than pasteurise: "Homogenising alters fat globules into a form our bodies are not equipped for. Research has found correlations between mass introduction of homogenised milk and increased heart disease." Campers, holiday-makers renting the self-catering cottages and other visitors can watch the milking.

The Evans' one-hundred-and-seventy-acre dairy and potato farm produces award-winning cheese, too. Wyn remembers his mother's stories of churning butter with her mother to take by rowboat to Pembroke market where it sold for three and a half old pence a pound; today, his daughter Linda makes cheddar and caerphilly by hand. The cheddar, aged up to eight months, is yellow in

The Evans produce the only unpasteurised, unhomogenised, organic milk in Wales, and sell it locally and in Chris's small shop to "a few discerning customers". Most customers won't touch it, fearing the raw milk's health risk "but," says Wyn, "benefits outweigh the risks; the heat of pasteurisation destroys enzymes which aid digestion, and destroys fifty per cent of the vitamin C."

summer when cows feast on fresh clover and paler in winter when they shelter in the barn. Three-week old caerphillies are creamy yet crumbly, with a pleasant tang. Once, they were made by hundreds of Welsh farmers' wives, including Wyn's grandmother. Buy them in the shop, open Whitsun to late September, or outlets in St David's. "Or ask your local deli to stock it...," says Wyn.

Plas Bodegroes

Efailnewydd Pwllheli
Gwynedd LL53 5TH
01758 612363 www.bodegroes.co.uk

"The Llyn Peninsula has never gone in for factory farming or for fertiliser," explains Plas Bodegroes' chef-patron Chris Chown. "Small farms have always supplied locally so everything is traceable and, despite having no badges, our whole area is, and always has been, I feel, organic with a small 'o'!"

Wrapped in roses, wisteria and a cast-iron veranda, with a heart in the lawn and a beech avenue, the Georgian restaurant with rooms is ridiculously romantic. It's also firmly off the beaten track in a wild corner of north-west Wales where the land flings itself into the Irish Sea. When

foie gras and also asparagus outside the UK season. "We try not to use African vegetables but I am tempted when there's nothing locally," he admits. There are good local crabs and lobsters, but fish is tricky. "There's no good halibut in the Irish Sea and if it comes from the North Sea it's two weeks old so we use farmed Norwegian. The quality is good because the fish have plenty of space. I also buy farmed Shetland sea trout for it seems a better alternative to massacring the last wild sea trout."

Chris's cooking is informed by common sense which he partly attributes to his mother, a Scottish-born

Chris and his Danish wife, Gunna, opened here, in 1986, Chris couldn't afford foreign ingredients and found it difficult to get them so he created original dishes, resurrected Welsh ones and hunted out local produce.

He claims to be one of very few chefs in Wales to only use native Welsh Black beef, two herds of which live on the peninsula; he buys dry-cured Carmarthen ham and bacon from a farmer four miles away rather than use Parma or Serrano ham; and he wind-dries their own lamb. He makes bread and can bake gluten-free and soda, but buys granary "because our baker does it better than us".

But Chris is pragmatic and honest about his sourcing. He is running a smart and respected restaurant (a Michelin star winner for over half its lifetime) and imports

domestic science teacher who, having grown up through the war, was naturally frugal. "It's insulting to the animal to throw any of it in the bin. With a duck, rather than just use the breasts, I'll use the neck to make sausages."

Unused meat from a roast leg of lamb will be cubed for kebabs; trimmings from sirloin will be added to kidney for a pie; spring turbot roe becomes taramasalata, and surplus seasonal fruit and vegetables become jams, chutneys, candied fruits, piccalilli or chutneys.

Chris dislikes categorising his style – "I have never knowingly followed a recipe " – but, as he is predominantly sourcing locally, he will concede to Modern Welsh. His dishes are unpretentious, simple and free of garnishes: breast of guinea fowl with mango and

celeriac, bara brith and butter pudding. And he sometimes looks abroad for inspiration. "The British have always been culinary magpies, great at stealing ideas. Devilled kidneys, that I serve with Welsh onion cakes, is nicked straight from Indian Raj breakfasts. If I find an amazing meal abroad, I'll do it at home with local ingredients." Hence his Thai dish, 'tom yam', a spicy hotpot he makes with local seafood.

Chris has a pathological hatred of waste. When they opened, they installed low energy light fittings as, he says, it seemed bonkers not to. Kitchen waste is composted for

"On a Sunday lunchtime, you will often only hear Welsh spoken – which I love!" Chris feels they have won local support not just because of their quality but also because their presence has genuinely improved the local economy. "I do feel part of the community. I'm vice-president of the local rugby club and I love walking across our grounds to the club on Saturday afternoons."

The refreshing thing about Chris in an age of celebrity chefs and fashionable environmentalism is that he is not afraid to go against the current zeitgeist. While many now dismiss nouvelle cuisine, he points out that it had its good

their herb and vegetable garden; polystyrene fish boxes are washed and returned to fishmongers; cardboard boxes returned to wine merchants.

Chris is bullish about his wine sourcing. "I stock around four-hundred bins and have to bite my lip when I think about the air miles, but you're never going to get good Burgundies growing on the Llyn Peninsula. I look for evidence of how close to their 'terroir' a grower is." He does stock three Welsh wines, Welsh whiskies, gin and spring water which he feels are the best of their kind.

He is proud that Bodegroes's staff, three chefs, furnishings and art are Welsh. It's a relaxed and intimate place, homely yet elegant, with a dining room that's supported by a good mix of locals and resident guests.

parts: "Putting fish on top of the sauce, rather than smothering it, was sensible". He recalls a remark made by Tom Jaine, the then editor of the Good Food Guide: "'Chefs as good as Chris Chown have no need to follow fashion'. That's the greatest compliment I've ever had."

Plas Bodegroes

Meal price: 4-course dinner, £42.50
Sunday lunch £18.50
No food Sunday evening or Monday evening
Nearest train: Pwllheli

Scotland

Key
Alastair Sawday's Special Places to eat
Soil Association certified organic producers

Map 7

Scotland

Cream o' Galloway

Rainton Gatehouse of Fleet Castle Douglas
Dumfries & Galloway DG7 2DR
01557 814040 www.creamogalloway.co.uk

Cream, milk, eggs, sugar and simple, natural ingredients to add flavour and texture... it's what you'd expect to see on the ingredients list of ice cream, but it's not normally what you'd find. Look on most ice cream cartons and you'll find vegetable fat, carrageenan, mono- and di-glycerides of fatty acids, locust bean gum, ammonium phosphatides and partially reconstituted whey protein. Note the conspicuous absence of cream.

Wilma Finlay runs an ice cream factory and visitor centre on a remote rugged farm in southwest Scotland; her ice creams, frozen yogurts and frozen smoothies are now so popular they are sold across the UK. "I've always studied food labels. Raspberry ice cream should contain cream, milk, eggs, sugar, real raspberries and not much else. Our ice creams are pale – the mint is not vivid green, the strawberry not lurid pink – because we don't add beetroot juice concentrate or other colourings. They're made with organic milk, a high proportion of cream and egg yolks to bind rather than emulsifiers and thickeners."

The Finlay family has ran the farm since 1927 and when Wilma gave up her corporate job in Glasgow to live here, they agreed to switch it to organic. Numbers of cattle and sheep were halved, giving them considerably more space both on the pastures and in the winter barns. When she arrived in the early nineties, Häagen Dazs had just revolutionised the market and the timing was ideal for another luxury natural product.

The Ayrshire cows are milked each morning at five o'clock and their milk travels just five hundred yards to the small factory where it is heated with cream, sugar

and yolks. This custard is then chilled, churned with flavourings and frozen. Modern equipment has eased the process, although Wilma finds it comes designed for liquid concentrates not real ingredients.

Dessert trends inspire flavours: caramel shortbread, crannachan (raspberries, honey, whisky and oatmeal), gingerbread, sticky toffee, banoffee, strawberry pavlova and honeycomb. Shortbread and chocolate cake are baked to her recipes by a local baker. Elderflower cordial has come from Belvoir Fruit Farms since Wilma simply ran out of hours in the day to make it herself. Meringue is whipped up in-house from organic eggs and fairtrade sugar. And Glen Moray single malt whisky comes from Wilma's native Elgin.

"I'd wanted everything to be organic, but not enough customers will pay for it," she says. "I wish people appreciated that organic farming is an excellent model for sustainable agriculture, and something that we will all need to support as fossil fuels deplete."

Visitors come between March and October for farm tours, tastings and comparisons of real and artificial vanilla, the latter more redolent of wax crayons and floor polish than the exquisitely perfumed orchid seed pod it attempts to emulate. Groups book in for 'Ready Steady Freeze' – the chance to create your own unique ice cream flavour - and are encouraged to explore the nature trails.

Visitors experience the difference between having thirty and ninety cows to a shed. "People don't realise most milk they drink comes from cows kept permanently cramped indoors," says Helen Fenby the centre manager. "After coming here many switch to organic milk."

Male calves, usually an unwanted by-product of the dairy industry, reach full adulthood here and are then slaughtered and the meat served in the tearoom. The Finlays hope to pioneer a new system which allows calves to wean naturally. "No farmer's wife is happy with the usual practice of taking them away after one day – it's heart-breaking. Leaving them together for a year, until the next calf arrives, will mean less milk for us but healthier, faster-growing, happier calves. It requires a complete overhaul of the dairy, but we're going to try."

Knockinaam Lodge

Portpatrick Stranraer
Dumfries & Galloway DG9 9AD
01776 810471 www.knockinaamlodge.com

Cooking here is a chef's dream. Every day Tony Pierce selects the freshest produce to create a five-course dinner for twenty guests. He's spoilt for choice. This too frequently overlooked corner of southwest Scotland quietly yields some of Britain's finest food: sea bass line-caught in Luce Bay, distinctively flavoured salt marsh lamb, roe deer from wild forests inland, redcurrants from Gulf Stream-warmed gardens.

"The set menu means diners can relax without having to make decisions. When there's choice, people tend to order grilled steak. Here, they try new things," explains owner David Ibbotson. Knockinaam's Michelin-starred food draws diners back again and again: one couple comes six times a year; local holiday homers return each summer; a not-so-Slow businessman regularly takes the twelve-minute helicopter ride from Belfast for lunch.

The remote setting is magnificent: sheltered by an arc of gorse-crested cliffs, the 1869 grey stone country house commands its own tiny cove at Dumfries and Galloway's westernmost tip, gazing out to Ireland and glorious sunsets. "Some years ago a TV programme about Skye took hundreds of thousands of visitors to the island. It was actually (and oddly) filmed here. The cameraman still comes for holidays, saying it's as magical as the islands, but without the crowds. People zip past on the motorway from Carlisle to Glasgow, not realising what beauty lies just to the west."

David and his wife Sian escaped here after years working for corporate hotel chains left David deadened by their lowest common denominator approach. "When we saw Knockinaam advertised we jumped at the chance to do something really special." Identikit breakfasts had particularly depressed David and now he proudly serves local black pudding, haggis and kippers, homemade muesli, muffins and marmalades, and John Mellis's renowned honey from nearby Auldgirth.

Originally owned by the Hunter-Blair baronets of Blairquhan Castle, this Victorian hunting lodge must have hosted hundreds of shooting parties. In its early days, feasts would have been French in flavour; Gallic culinary influence following James V's marriage to Mary of Guise-Lorraine held strong for centuries. Today, Tony's classical training returns French finesse to the table, while the Ibbotsons create a house party atmosphere.

In the candlelit dining room, roast fillet of Angus beef with pommes Anna might be followed by a pear tart with calvados ice cream and vanilla sabayon. "Dishes are quite simple, their strength is in their flavours not fussy presentation," says David, who loathes formal hotel dining. Everything is made from scratch, from crisps laid

out on the bar to breakfast croissants; ice creams and sorbets come in myriad flavours and Tony's petit four repertoire is fifty-strong.

Local seafood is on the end of Tony's filleting knife within hours of swimming in the Irish Sea: sweet langoustine ravioli scattered with hazelnut praline and lemon oil; native crab paired with fresh ginger in gazpacho; dived scallops seared with Italian ham. David and Tony catch pollack, bass and mackerel from the hotel's beach.

Sunday lunch will see more meat on the menu. "The dairy farming community here has never much liked fish – one reason there's still plenty around," explains David. Butcher Alex Jack in Stranraer supplies local lamb, free-range chicken and Aberdeen Angus beef. In season Tony makes pheasant terrines, roasts partridge and grouse (the latter native to the Scottish moors, the meat delicately flavoured by the herbs they eat) and favours tender roe deer fillets over more powerful red deer venison.

The cheeseboard is sublime with Dunsyre Blue from Lanarkshire, Isle of Mull cheddar, Cairnsmore, a hard goat's cheese made thirty miles away, and award-winning biodynamic cheeses from Loch Arthur, a social enterprise near Dumfries which provides a working community for adults with special needs.

The surprisingly balmy climate suits gardener Sandy Murray, whose early potatoes, broad beans, peas, shallots, leeks, artichokes and more fill expanding beds. "Root vegetables store well but they taste infinitely better freshly harvested," he says. Manure provides natural fertility, while salty air deters slugs. There's also an abundant peach tree in the greenhouse and David's five-hundred wines and one-hundred-and-sixty single malts to reward the traveller who leaves the motorway and heads west.

Knockinaam Lodge

Five-course tasting menu £55 p.p.
Best meal deal: 4-course Sunday lunch, £29.50
Meals always available
Nearest train: Stranraer

Windlestraw Lodge

Galashiels Road Walkerburn
Scottish Borders EH43 6AA
01896 870636 www.windlestraw.co.uk

For over thirty years Alan and Julie Reid have been in the business of pleasing people – Alan as chef and Julie as front of house in hotels and pubs. Brought up in Berwickshire and trained in Scotland, Alan did stints in big hotels and city restaurants before running his own, highly successful pub with Julie in the Borders; together they transformed it into a restaurant–with–rooms and swiftly won recognition.

After seventeen years, though, they began hankering "after a house with a view and white table cloths in the dining room – something more traditional." That was in 2003. "We were becoming disillusioned when we ate out," recalls Alan. "Everything was miniscule portions – 'art on the plate' – and I wanted to bring people honest food again. I wanted to have time to make our own jams and breads, too."

Within a year they fell for the charms of Windlestraw Lodge, a handsome stone Edwardian house on the banks of the river Tweed built as a wedding present by a mill-owner for his wife.

Their timing coincided with a growth in the number of small-scale, local producers who could give Alan all the local raw materials he so coveted: Aberdeen Angus beef (hung for twenty-one days) from Hardiesmill Farm near Gordon; organic Tamworth pork and bacon and organic rose veal, from Peelham Farm at Foulden. Organic vegetables and hand-picked mushrooms come from growers in East Lothian while flour, oats and barley come from Heatherslaw Mill in Northumberland.

Fish and shellfish are landed at nearby Eyemouth and the area is teeming with game – grouse from the Buccleuch Estate, partridge from the Lammermuirs, roe deer from the Tweed valley forest.

Alan is no mean hunter himself and enjoys fishing and shooting; his forays in Speyside often have him returning with half a dozen red deer for the freezer.

Fruit, herbs and salad leaves come from their, or from friends', gardens. "We've got friends with an apple and pear orchard that is over one-hundred years old. The trees have never been sprayed." Alan admits they could grow more vegetables but the deer often put paid to their plans – "I'd rather look at deer than have extra vegetables, though."

"Our emphasis is on local and seasonal produce, so if I can't buy it from a local producer then it doesn't feature on the menu. In the heart of winter, I may occasionally have to buy the odd ingredient from other producers, but rarely."

Daily-changing menus depend on local catches or shoots. "Suppliers turn up unexpectedly, too," says Alan, "and the menu can change up to ten times before dinner, much to Julie's frustration, as I muse on ideas and combinations." While walking he may spot brambles and chanterelles and on his return will add crumble and risotto to the menu.

"My food is honest; I won't 'flower up' dishes," says Alan. "The simplest way is the best, to maintain flavour."

He never writes down a recipe – "well, there's no other chef in the kitchen, so there's no point," he says, reasonably. "I might make pumpkin soup with honey and ginger one day, but the next day with orange." The cooking is confident and accomplished: wood pigeon with black pudding and crisp pancetta, for example, or sea bass on a tomato, spring onion and basil salsa.

Virtually everything is made from scratch: bread, oatcakes, fruit compôtes, marmalades, preserves, sorbets, biscuits and petits fours. And how many restaurant kitchens have an Aga? The Reids installed one so they could let dishes, such as braised oxtails and duck confit, cook gently and undisturbed.

As Alan works his quiet magic in the kitchen, guests and diners gather for drinks and canapés in the comfortable sitting room that's warmed by a log fire in the winter. The house, although substantial, has been given a lightness of touch in its furnishings which makes it intimate rather than intimidating. People spruce up rather than dress up for dinner and, after a drink or two, tend to fall into conversation.

If they're very busy, Julie might be helped by a couple of local girls but the style of service is unfussy – you pour your own wine (organic and biodynamic) and genuinely relax. There are just six tables in the polished-floored, wood-panelled dining room and eating here is

like taking part in a house party where everyone, hosts included, are enjoying themselves.

By the time guests leave, particularly if they've stayed overnight – and Alan's poached smoked haddock with an egg on top for breakfast is sublime – people are transformed. "Often when they arrive they don't say much," says Alan. "When they leave they are relaxed and happy. That's what we like!"

Windlestraw Lodge

Set dinner £44.50
Private dining parties welcome
Food served seven days a week
Nearest train: Edinburgh

"Our output isn't just food, it's the relationships, learning and fun too," says Pete Ritchie. He and partner Heather Anderson sell their beef, lamb, pork, eggs, fruit and vegetables to a loyal crowd through their shop, café and local delivery scheme, while uncompromisingly promoting their organic farming philosophy and helping reinvent the local food system.

When Pete and Heather stumbled across the 'for sale' sign twenty miles south-west of Edinburgh, they were ready for a new challenge. They sealed the deal and immediately began organic conversion.

"Before, as community workers in Edinburgh, we challenged conventional notions about disability; now we're doing the same about food. Organic farming is

rejected as unsuitable for the mechanised processes. "For all we knew our meat ended up on shelves down the road, yet untraceable to Whitmuir. We wanted to take control and know our customers."

A gift of two Tamworth sows – Cinnamon and Nutmeg, thought to be sterile yet proving prolific – spurred the move to direct sales. A tiny shop was swapped for a bigger one and now they have a restaurant, too. "We invested everything and have more risk and direct accountability to consumers, but we wouldn't go back to anonymous wholesale."

Nearly two-hundred households – all within twenty-five miles and most within five – pay a monthly fixed amount of their choice. They email orders or pop in to the

about restraint. We should only take what we need, not all that's possible or desirable. We respect nature, the soil and those who work it."

At first cattle and lambs were trucked four-hundred miles to a slaughter house in Devon, from where meat travelled to supermarkets across Britain. If supply outstripped demand, orders were reduced or delayed without notice. If animals grew too large, they were

shop, and accounts are settled quarterly. This fixed income, one third of total sales, is hugely reassuring, especially on a wet weekday when the shop is empty. Members attend events – artisan chocolate-making demos, jam and chutney swaps, talks on pig and poultry welfare, beekeeping, 'real' bread and fairtrade.

Most join us because they want local food. "But," says Peter, "'local' is no guarantee of quality. There's a

farm nearby with over a million chickens – five per cent of the UK's laying flock – in giant sheds. On a good day several hundred make it outdoors, so he can call them 'free-range'. There's little that is good about those 'local' eggs."

Whitmuir's Shorthorn cattle eat only grass. This gives their meat a healthier balance of Omega-6s to Omega-3s, and softer, yellower fat. Calves also wean naturally. An early attempt to hasten the process by luring calves away to a field of tasty kale resulted in disaster when they trashed three electric fences and a gate to reclaim their young. Pigs live in family groups, too, and in summer sows build nests in the woods to farrow. If discovered, a sow will move her piglets to another secret location, so strong is her protective instinct. "This isn't an efficient

Resident butchers, septuagenarian Jeremiah Sinclair (a fifth generation master butcher) and his "glamorous assistant" twenty-two-year-old Philippa Mueller, run a bespoke service in a sixteenth-century barn. A bakery with wood-burning oven is next, to be financed through 'bread bonds' and serve as a community resource. With no organic stone-ground flour available locally, Pete is planning to bring together cereal farmers, bakers and millers to see if they can change this.

In the café, food is all organic. "Either it matters or it doesn't so we're one-hundred per cent organic, not just 'organic when possible'," says Pete. The café has ten-inch thick sheep wool insulation, low-carbon concrete, a ground source heat pump and a wood-burning stove.

way to produce pork, but it's a fantastic way to educate, and the meat is more flavoursome."

Ignoring experts' advice that they were too high, cold, wet and windy to grow veg, Pete and Heather grow beans, courgettes, root vegetables and soft fruits by 'alley cropping'. Plots are separated by rows of trees that shelter vegetables and encourage biodiversity, provide wood to sell and yield hazelnuts, crab apples and rowan berries.

Whitmuir goes way beyond carbon neutral: it is twenty-five per cent woodland and the Ritchies donate money to a tree-planting project to offset livestock methane emissions.

Their approach is about more than 'local food for local people'. "International trade needs to be fairer, with less going through the multinationals who control so much. 'Food sovereignty' is vital, particularly in developing countries. We need to rethink food policy at all levels."

Pillars of Hercules

Falkland Cupar
Fife KY15 7AD
01337 857749   www.pillars.co.uk

"Topical issues change: animal welfare, health, global warming. But organic principles stay the same: using natural systems to produce food, rather than fighting nature with artificial inputs." Bruce Bennett has farmed organically in Fife since 1983, when the concept was alien to many. His mixed farm has grown from two to twenty-five acres, neighbouring farms have converted, and his vegetable box scheme expanded during the recession.

"In the last ten years there's been a huge surge of interest in food provenance and environmental issues. More people want organic food, local food they can trust, and alternatives to supermarkets," says Bruce, whose store has matured from a lean-to shed with an honesty box to a bustling shop and café with community events and popular dinners.

"The organic movement is a cultural one, too. In the last fifty years the rural workforce has been decimated. When I arrived, Falkland was a bigger village and there were a number of independent food shops. Now there's one and villages are full of commuters. The few farmers left spend their days driving enormous combines; it apparently makes more sense for society to have two million unemployed rather than working in 'uneconomic' jobs on the land. These aren't healthy changes."

Eighteen people are employed here – way above the farm average – and staff and apprentices of all ages help with polytunnels of beans, potatoes, celery, garlic, fennel, kale, salad leaves, strawberries and herbs. Growing such a variety is hard work - plots are too small for mechanisation - but it allows for effective crop rotation to keep soil healthy and fertile. It keeps the customers happy, too. Laying hens roam in the expanding apple orchards - Bruce tries to plant another fifty trees each year - and Christmas turkeys peck over clover-rich grass. "Customers order our Bronzes year after year. They taste great as they get exercise and eat a variety of natural foods, including vegetable scraps."

Bruce learnt the hard way that offering only potatoes and turnips in winter soon loses custom. So alongside his produce in the shop sit meats, cheeses, fruits and vegetables from farms further afield. While the vast majority is organic, Bruce does support local entrepreneurs such as Jane Stewart who makes crumbly farmhouse Anster cheese and Your Piece bakery that makes handmade oatcakes.

The café spills out of the timber-framed shop, built with old telegraph poles, onto a rustic veranda. Walkers and shoppers "who avoid supermarkets" flock here. Once or twice a month, local chef Christopher Trotter, Slow Food supporter and author of several Scottish cookbooks, comes. Shop shelves are wheeled away, extra tables laid, candles lit and a jazz ensemble installed for a merry band of locals eager to feast on Christopher's beetroot bubble and squeak, leek and potato cakes with celery and apple salsa and summer fruit bread and butter pudding. Two out of three mains options are meat-free.

People come to pick their own flowers, too, which particularly pleases Bruce as it encourages creativity to make the most of what is on offer: "Floristry is an horrendous industry - supplying flowers flown half-way round the world, quite possibly grown with sprays in places where workers are not protected from the health risks," he says. "As with food, we must get away from the idea that we can have whatever we want whenever."

"The organic movement
is a cultural one, too.
In the last fifty years
the rural workforce
has been decimated"

Wark Farm
Cushnie Alford
Aberdeenshire AB33 8LL
01975 581149 www.warkfarm.co.uk

Dugie and Jenny Foreman, trained ecologists both, came here initially with the aim of encouraging wildlife. The cattle were introduced only to manage the grassland and, thereby, lure more birdlife. "The Belted Galloway cattle's grazing can be timed to create perfect conditions for waders, skylarks and other birds. So we brought them in and when we decided to offer the locals the beef, they were keen but pushed us to produce pork too."

So pigs joined the cattle and the birds did indeed come: nesting snipe, grey partridge and lapwings, among others. The call of the snipe circling its territory on their land is music to the Foremans' ears.

Breeds were chosen to suit the harsh conditions. Belted Galloway cows are short and stocky and graze outside year-round; Hebridean sheep are equally hardy and their wool is sent to the Isle of Mull to be woven into traditional tweed. The Oxford, Sandy and Black pigs are hairy enough to stand the cold and rain. All the meat produced is butchered onsite to organic standards.

"Animals here live longer than the norm," says Dugie, "and the meat is richer, tastier and with better distributed fat. Animals are not pushed to grow fast, which means less stress and disease and cattle can be entirely grass-fed, which is better for their health and ours. Growing our own feed protects us from the oscillating price of grain."

There are geese, too – the only certified organic flock in Scotland – that range free, forage and have access to water to do what they love most: ducking their heads under to shoot water over their backs. They live to six months and are stunned before slaughter, dry-plucked and hung for at least ten days.

"Most geese in British supermarkets are imported and were reared in sheds. They were wet-plucked, which means they cannot be hung, so won't have the same depth of flavour; the wetter the bird the less its skin will crispen in the oven," explains Dugie.

Dugie and Jenny taught themselves curing

techniques to utilise less popular cuts: smoked and unsmoked bacons and hams, duck rillettes, corned beef and more. There's a continental charcuterie range, too: Italian pancetta, French andouille sausage (garlicky and smokey), German leberwurst (spreadable pork liver sausage). The smoker uses beech chips rather than the usual oak, creating a subtle flavour that reminds Dugie of smoking fish by the river as a child.

While the Foremans will happily courier their meat across Britain, they prefer to know their customers personally. Most buy direct from the farm on open days (the last Thursday, Friday and Saturday of each month), sign up for the central Aberdeenshire delivery scheme or find Dugie and Jenny at a farmers' market.

"We are not a shop; we manage the whole supply chain and keep it short," says Dugie, who trained to be a butcher; Jenny makes the charcuterie. "People are buying more than a lump of protein, they're getting reassurance and a connection to the farm. Many care about animal welfare, some want foods untainted by agrichemicals and others simply appreciate the taste. Good chefs visit before buying; I'm not interested in those who don't."

Dugie offers tours and tastings, supports his local Slow Food convivium, and makes time to do talks at schools, sometimes with piglets in tow to the delight of squealing children.

"We'll only move to a more sustainable localised food system if there's a huge cultural shift in buying and eating habits," he says. "People are unwittingly perpetuating a cruel and carbon-heavy industrial meat system so producers like us need to engage, enthuse and educate."

The Spotty Pig pork pies do a good job of exciting local enthusiasm. "No secret recipe, no unusual spices, just top quality ingredients," says Dugie. "Having spent many hard hours in the fields looking after the animals to make excellent meat, why would I disguise it? Many people douse meat with strong flavours because it's so bland. They might as well use tofu."

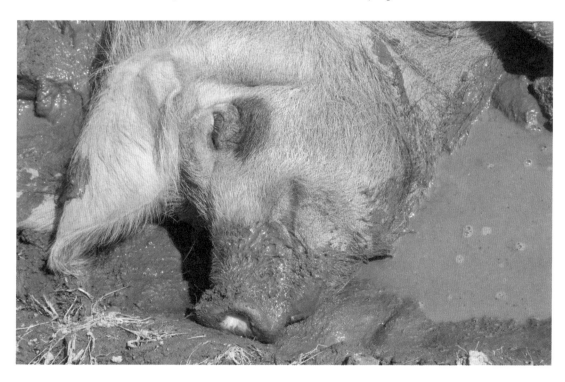

Black Isle Brewery

Old Allangrange Munlochy
Ross-shire IV8 8NZ
01463 811871 www.blackislebrewery.com

A little road that winds through a golden valley swaying with organic barley takes you to David Gladwin's brewery. The Black Isle – a particularly fertile peninsula off north-east Scotland – is a corner of Scotland long associated with brewing. When David arrived some thirty years ago breweries had long-since disappeared, yet all the ingredients were still there: delicious pure Highlands water, lush fields of barley and a maltings just over the Beauly Firth in Inverness. They say neccesity is the mother of invention and, with a family to feed and a roof to replace, David hit on the idea of reviving the area's beer-making history.

A series of historical revelations bolstered his resolve. During renovations of his farmhouse remnants of eighteenth-century brewing were unearthed, which prompted David to dig further in local archives. The house had been built by Sir Roderick McKenzie, one of the first to cultivate grain on the peninsula. The name of the house derives from the Gaelic 'allan-chrain', meaning 'fertile field of corn'. An old glass bottle seal bearing the name,

dug up by his cocker spaniel, sealed the deal.

"We've been organic since the start. I had seen too many vast monocrops doused in chemicals just when wildlife was in full bloom. It's no wonder bees are keeling over. Organic beer is more expensive – organic barley costs me twice as much as conventional, hops treble – but it makes a real difference to our countryside."

Black Hebridean sheep feed on spent malt and in return fertilise the barley fields, while keeping family and friends in sweet, rich meat and fleeces as soft as cashmere. Hens peck for stray grains, and their cow, another malt fan, produces prodigious quantities of milk for homemade cheese, butter and clotted cream. A three-hundred-foot borehole supplies the brewery's water, while a reed bed system cleverly returns effluent safely to the land. "It is The Good Life," says David.

Visitors come to see the different stages of beer-making: the infusion of malted barley in the 'mash tun', the boiling of the resulting 'wort' in the 'copper' with aromatic hops, fermenting, conditioning and bottling.

"Kiln-drying malt is akin to coffee bean roasting,"

says David, who encourages visitors to smell the differences: dark 'coffee' and 'chocolate' roasts for the rich porter and stouts; lighter malts for the pale ale and lager styles; aromatic toasty 'crystal' malt, everyone's favourite, used in the powerful Scotch ale.

Many of the beers are bottle conditioned. Using a German technique called 'kräusening', akin to the méthode Champenoise, live fermenting beer is added for a second fermentation inside the bottle. The result is a naturally sparkling beer which develops in character. The dead yeast settles at the bottom of the bottle, the sign of a real ale and a conscience-salving source of vitamin B.

David incorporates local flavours: oatmeal enriches the Hibernator stout; peat-smoked whisky malt enhances the Scotch ale; highland heather honey balances hoppy bitterness in another. Many pair well with Scottish food: Belgian-style wheat beer with mussels, porter with raw oysters or cheddar, Scotch ale with haggis. All can be bought direct, at independent off-licences and online.

"The system of globalised industrial agriculture is crazy – for example, one year, the price of barley more than halved. We need to create markets for small producers," insists David. "We get up at four every Saturday morning to drive to Edinburgh farmers' market. We small guys can't afford to sit back."

Scarista House

Scarista Isle of Harris
Western Isles HS3 3HX
01859 550238 www.scaristahouse.com

Three miles of alabaster beach and turquoise sea stretch out in front of the Hebridean white-washed Georgian manse. A lunar landscape of windswept treeless hills rises behind, dotted with hardy Blackface sheep. In summer, when the Isle of Harris is light beyond midnight, the setting sun lights up Scarista: walls glow pink and windows flash incandescent across the Sound of Taransay.

"The stunning, remote setting and the tightly woven small community attracted us," say Tim and Patricia Martin, who bought the hotel in 1999 having known and loved the island for twenty years. "We left our restaurant in London and were immediately welcomed into the community, not least because we continued to employ local staff and use local suppliers."

"I love the sense of immediacy, knowing where food is from, how it was produced, sensing its integrity and tasting its freshness," says Tim.

Creel-caught langoustines, lobsters and dived scallops from the Minch and fish landed at Stornoway are menu regulars. Tim makes gallons of fish stock to create classic French sauces with generous quantities of cream, butter, white Burgundy and fresh herbs. Scallops come on Jerusalem artichoke puree with a vinaigrette of clarified butter, vanilla and reduced sherry vinegar; turbot with sauce vièrge; John Dory on creamy saffron risotto.

"There are sustainability issues with some Atlantic trawled fish, but I'm reluctant to source from further afield as I won't compromise on freshness and quality. Unfortunately I can't get line-caught fish as most fishermen now have bigger boats. Farmed fish could be an option, but it takes a lot of small wild fish to feed them." It has been said that it can take three to four kilograms of small fish to create one kilogram of farmed salmon.

Smoked fish – "the best in the world" – comes from Inverawe and North and South Uist: undyed kippers for buttered toast, and flaky hot-smoked salmon for a scrambled egg breakfast; peat-smoked salmon on black ale blinis; smoked scallops with cauliflower velouté for dinner. Smoking fish originated here as a method for preserving salmon that had spawned and passed their prime; a 'kipper' was a spawning salmon.

But sourcing locally is not always possible. "There's no real 'farming' on the Outer Hebrides, and the growing season is short. Plus we have the challenge of varying our menus for those who stay a week or two." So extra

supplies arrive from the mainland such as poultry, pork and Aberdeen Angus beef.

Several hundred miles further north than Moscow, local fruit and vegetables are hardest to source. Organic gardener Annik Merlin manages to coax strawberries, raspberries, chard, courgettes, peas and more under polytunnels, and the Martins grow herbs and salad leaves. But there are not enough local growers to meet hotels' demand. Frustratingly, it is difficult to benefit from neighbouring Skye's food renaissance as transportation companies insist on going via Inverness and Stornoway.

Game, though, is abundant in season. "A vivid childhood memory is waking to the sound of my father shooting pigeons from his bedroom window as they raided our kitchen garden! So it's a special pleasure to serve roasted wood pigeon, with bread sauce and buttered crumbs, just as my mother did," says Tim. Fried crumbs are also churned into delicious brown bread ice cream, served with port syrup and roasted figs.

The fantastic George MacLeod has been at the hotel for twenty years and runs front of house. A Hearach, born and raised a mile away, he will share his vast knowledge of local history, culture and language. His mother Flora was one of the last on Harris to make crowdie – naturally soured and curdled raw cow's milk. This soft cheese, once Islanders' standard breakfast, became scarce during the Clearances, when mass sheep-farming was introduced and crofters lost their traditional way of life.

But with no television, and miles of space and tranquillity all around, this still feels like the kind of place where things are still done the 'slow' way: Tim and Patricia make granola, yogurt, marmalade, ice creams, pasta, cakes and breads themselves. They also make petits fours, Highland heather honey chocolate truffles and mini shortbread jammy dodgers and are considering trying crowdie. Traditional oatcakes are cooked by George's mother on her cast iron griddle, to her secret recipe.

George expertly oversees the cheeseboard: Isle of Mull cheddar, Dunsyre Blue from South Lanarkshire, Grimbister from Orkney, washed rind Criffel from Dumfries and brie-style Clava from Inverness. "The occasional Irish cheese makes it onto George's board, but he leaves English ones at the back of the fridge!" says Tim.

Scarista House

Set 3-course dinner with canapés, £40
Set 4-course dinner with canapés, £49.50
Dinner available every evening March–December
No trains on Harris, but regular ferries here

Useful and interesting websites

Food and farming issues

www.soilassociation.org
Membership charity campaigning for planet-friendly, sustainable and healthy food and farming systems.

www.soilassociation.org/certification
UK's leading certification body certifying around 80% of organic produce.

www.slowfood.com
International eco-gastronomic organisation founded in Italy to counteract fast food and fast life.

www.slowfood.org.uk
Slow Food in the UK – join your local convivium to take part in events and learn more about 'good, clean and fair food'.

www.sustainweb.org
The alliance for better food and farming – campaigns, food facts, news, local networks and more.

www.msc.org
The Marine Stewardship Council certifies sustainable seafood – look out for their blue label.

www.fishonline.org
Look up your seafood choices to check sustainability issues before buying.

www.fish2fork.com
Find restaurants serving sustainable seafood and shame those who don't – site by Charles Clover, author of The End of the Line.

www.foodethicscouncil.org
Thought-provoking discussion on food poverty, air freight, climate change and water scarcity.

www.ciwf.org.uk
Compassion in World Farming campaigns to end cruel factory farming and to encourage us all to eat less meat.

www.rbst.org.uk
Rare Breeds Survival Trust – look up breeds at risk and find accredited butchers.

www.biodynamic.org.uk
Information on biodynamic farming and gardening and the Demeter certification label.

www.foodforlife.org.uk
Network of schools and communities across England committed to transforming food culture.

www.fairtrade.org.uk
Fairtrade food, Fairtrade schools, Fairtrade towns, Fairtrade fortnight and more.

www.gmwatch.org
Latest news on the issue of genetically modified (GM) food and crops.

www.lovefoodhatewaste.com
8.3 million tonnes of food is thrown away by UK households every year. Tips and recipes for leftovers to help you waste less.

www.makinglocalfoodwork.co.uk
Connecting community groups and farmers to increase access to fresh, healthy, local food with clear, traceable origins.

www.fifediet.co.uk
Network of people trying to re-localise their food, not only in Fife!

www.climatefriendlyfood.org.uk
Comprehensive carbon calculator for farmers, and the world's first low-carbon food certification scheme.

Growing your own

www.landshare.net
Hugh Fearnley-Whittingstall's initiative to connect landowners with veg growers.

www.gardenorganic.org.uk
Organic gardening advice, courses, events, heritage seed library and resources for schools.

www.askorganic.co.uk
Scotland's experts on organic gardening.

www.organicgarden.org.uk
More organic gardening news, views, interviews and support.

www.downtheallotment.co.uk
Connect with other plot-holders on your allotment site.

www.allotment.org.uk
Advice on growing and cooking vegetables and fruits, including information on keeping chickens.

www.wwoof.org.uk
World Wide Opportunities on Organic Farms – volunteer on a farm, smallholding or garden to connect with the soil and gain skills.

www.naturalbeekeepingtrust.org
Promotes awareness of the ways of keeping bees that respects the nature and needs of the bees.

Celebrating British food

www.eattheseasons.co.uk
Find out what's good to eat right now in the UK.

www.foodloversbritain.com
Virtual food fair, promoting high quality local food businesses.

www.gourmetbritain.com
Guide to the best of British gourmet food, including an encyclopaedia of food terms.

www.localfoodadvisor.com
Find award-winning producers, suppliers and farmers markets.

www.greatbritishkitchen.co.uk
The British Food Trust's guide to seasonal recipes, regional cooking, culinary traditions and food history.

www.bigbarn.co.uk
Find seasonal and local food.

www.farmshopping.net
Find your nearest farm shop.

www.farmersmarkets.net
Find your nearest farmers' market.

www.specialistcheesemakers.co.uk
Search for specialist and traditional cheeses around Britain.

www.realbreadcampaign.org
Find outlets selling bread full of natural ingredients and free from artificial additives.

Blogs

www.allotment2kitchen.blogspot.com
Vegetarian adventures in a Scottish allotment and kitchen.

www.mytinyplot.co.uk
A kitchen garden and keen cook in Bath.

www.britishfoodanddrink.blogspot.com
A guide to the best seasonal food, with recipe tips.

www.cottagesmallholder.com
A couple's journey towards their goal of partial self-sufficiency.

www.britishlarder.co.uk
Recipes and more from a professional chef.

www.bakingforbritain.blogspot.com
Regional specialities and traditional ingredients in the cake, biscuit and bun line.

www.thefreshloaf.com
Online community of amateur artisan bakers and bread enthusiasts, including online lessons and active forum.

www.tracingpaper.org.uk
A piecemeal investigation into the origins of our food.

www.foodpolitics.com
Writer Marion Nestle's blog about issues such as school food, obesity and food labelling.

www.realfoodlover.wordpress.com
Journalist Elizabeth Winkler's blog on food politics and home cooking.

www.honest-food.net
Story of an American hunter, angler, gardener and cook, including recipes for curing meat and preserving produce.

www.culinaryanthropologist.org
This book's author's slow food adventures. Stories, recipes, classes.

www.kenalbala.blogspot.com
The culinary experiments of a food historian.

www.languageoffood.blogspot.com
Fascinating essays on the language of food.

Further reading

www.michaelpollan.com
A man full of good food sense. The Omnivore's Dilemma and In Defense of Food might just change your life.

www.nigelslater.com
And one with good cooking sense. Seasonal, simple and delicious.

The Taste of Britain
by Laura Mason and Catherine Brown
A weighty compendium of all that is great about regional British food, from Arbroath smokies to Yorkshire parkin.

Economy Gastronomy:
Eat Better and Spend Less
by Allegra McEvedy and Paul Merrett
A fantastic cookbook that includes meal and menu planning, store-cupboard basics and great approachable recipes. As does...

The Art of Simple Food:
Notes, Lessons and Recipes from a Delicious Revolution
by Alice Waters

Riverford Farm Cook Book:
Tales from the Fields,
Recipes from the Kitchen
by Guy Watson and Jane Baxter
A brilliant resource for using up your weekly vegetable box.

Taste: The Story of Britain through its Cooking
by Kate Colquhoun
Charts the fascinating history of British food, as does the next...

British Food: An extraordinary thousand years of history
by Colin Spencer

www.fireandknives.com
Quarterly magazine of new writing about food – culture, history, nerdy facts and short stories. For the food lover's library, not the kitchen.

www.forkmagazine.com
'Real food' enthusiasts – news, markets, restaurants and recipes.

The Soil Association's Organic Farm Schools

Breathe deeply, connect with nature, nurture your soul, learn a new skill. The Soil Association has set up an Organic Farm School for those interested in growing their own food, rearing animals, cooking, baking and rural crafts. They are all held on working organic farms.

A Soil Association survey found that ninety-two per cent of people in the UK believe in the importance of educating people in growing food and rearing livestock. And yet just at the time when we'd like to connect with the soil and learn how to be more self-sufficient, our confidence in being able to do so is at an all-time low. Those who decide to rise to the challenge and learn a few gardening skills will be disappointed to find that the average waiting list for an allotment is over three years.

The Soil Association, with the support of the Daylesford Foundation, aims to restore our confidence and to boost our skill-set. Join in and you will learn practical skills directly from experienced organic farmers, growers and producers, each of whom has a real passion for education. With over three-hundred courses to choose from, everyone can find inspiration.

The Daylesford Foundation that helps fund the Organic Farm Schools promotes sustainable, organic farming and its core belief is that soil is sacred.

Daylesford Farm in Gloucestershire began its organic life over twenty years ago and its founder, Carol Bamford, is inspired by India's craft-orientated village economy.

"The Foundation is dedicated to supporting the precious skills of the artisan and aims to support those who promote sustainability in agriculture, in manufacture and in individual communities," she says. "It can help to create things of real value and permanence in a transient and industrialised world."

Twenty-six other farms in the UK are now part of the Organic Farm School scheme and courses include dry stone walling, hedge laying, chicken keeping, pig rearing, foraging, sausage-making, curing, brewing, fruit preserving, cheese-making, and many organic growing and gardening courses.

You can unleash your creativity, too, as you learn to identify, pick and arrange wild flowers, build bird boxes and weave willow. There are also courses for those longing to be a smallholder: how to set up and manage a smallholding; how to choose and keep cattle; sheep care and handling; how to lamb successfully. Particularly inspiring are lectures on permaculture and biodynamic farming that draw on the inspirational philosophies of Rudolf Steiner.

The Soil Association hopes to foster compassion towards animals, create lasting harmony between our soil and us and to reach over three-thousand individuals. Go and embrace Slow in all its forms, have fun and immerse yourself in a new and enriching experience.

For more details visit www.soilassociation.org and search for 'Organic Farm School'

The Soil Association

Be the change. Join the movement.
Join today by visiting
www.soilassociation.org/joinus

Join the Soil Association from as little as £2 a month

The Soil Association is a membership charity campaigning for planet-friendly food and farming. It believes in the connection between soil, food, the health of people and the health of the planet.

Your support will help it:

Say 'no' to Genetically Modified foods
The Soil Association led the way in persuading supermarkets to adopt a No-GM Policy. It is now campaigning to stop GM products being introduced without our knowing, for example via animal feed.

Promote local food
The Soil Association supports local food projects that bring producers and consumers together, and encourages people to cook and grow their own food.

Improve conditions for farm animals
The Soil Association's organic standards prohibit factory farming and guarantee truly free-range conditions and high standards of animal welfare.

Members receive:

- Quarterly editions of the Soil Association's magazine 'Living Earth'

- Access to organic offers at hundreds of retail outlets

- Up to 25% discount on Organic Farm School courses on which you can learn traditional skills such as brewing, meat curing, bee-keeping and foraging

- Invitations to fun days out on the farms in its organic network and discounted or free tickets to festivals and events

  Membership costs from just £2 a month. To join on-line go to www.soilassociation.org or call the membership team on 0117 914 2447

 **Soil Association**

Soil Association
South Plaza
Marlborough Street
Bristol BS1 3NX
Registered charity no. 206862 (England and Wales)
Registered charity no. SC039168 (Scotland)

Triodos Bank

Triodos Bank's motives are as decent as one can find: it lends ONLY to organisations and companies that it considers to be making a positive contribution to the planet and the community. Many organic farms and projects have benefited from loans from Triodos and lending to these brings particular pleasure for the legacy of their practices is one that has far-reaching and long-lasting benefits.

Triodos has a refreshingly different and slow approach to money... Whatever your approach, you will agree it is hard to avoid money, whether you are acquiring, spending or saving it. It is in constant flow and, like electricity, you can't benefit directly from it, only from what it can do for you. We've become used to it being reduced to numbers on a page and to believe that nothing matters other than the rate of return. We don't always consider who will bear the consequences of our earning high rates of return. By entrusting money to a bank, we wash our hands of it. It's just a mechanism for multiplying money until we need to use it.

In contrast, it's difficult to find anybody discussing how money will make you feel but when it is used for purposes that we feel good about – helping people, rewarding work, educating, and unlocking potential – then we can enjoy it and feel spiritually prosperous. We need to consider money as an extension of ourselves and direct it for the purposes that we choose.

Triodos Bank was conceived in 1968, when four friends – an economist, a professor, a consultant and a banker – formed a study group. These men, inspired by student protests round the world and the work of Austrian social thinker Rudolf Steiner, debated how money could be handled in a socially-conscious way. They wanted finance to act in a way that values community, culture and the environment, as well as profit. Today, Triodos is the world's leading sustainable bank, with funds under management of over £4 billion and lending to over 12,500 ethical organisations, including seven-hundred in the UK. It has branches in the UK, The Netherlands, Belgium, Spain and Germany, and through its pioneering microfinance work, providing finance for millions of poorer people in the developing world, the Bank's influence is global.

The financial crisis has demonstrated the inherent unsustainability of a global financial system obsessed by the 'fast buck'. By contrast, what an enterprise sets out to do, and what motivates the people behind it, are the Bank's first consideration, examined before a loan's financial viability is considered. The projects that make the grade are in areas ranging from renewable energy and recycling to fair trade, organic farming, community groups and village shops.

A loan from Triodos helped, for example, Ben and Charlotte Hollins from Shropshire hold on to Fordhall, their family farm. In 2004 the brother and sister inherited the farm from their father, an organic pioneer who had managed it as a tenant farmer sustainably since the Second World War. When the owner of Fordhall wanted to sell it, possibly to developers, the Hollins raised funds themselves and launched a community shareholding initiative. Triodos Bank made up the shortfall and Fordhall became the first community-owned farm in England. There are plans for an educational centre and a bunkhouse so that young people from inner cities can experience first hand the pasture-to-plate cycle.

There's even an eco-publisher or two in there. A loan from Triodos Bank helped Alastair Sawday's dream of having one of the UK's most environmentally friendly offices become a reality in 2006.

Triodos Bank is the only commercial bank in the UK to publish details of everyone it lends money to so savers can understand the benefits their money brings.

Fast money, like fast food, is full of empty calories. Money only starts to have true value when you know your financial choices match the values by which you live your life. Investing well is rather like buying organic food: it may not be the cheapest or most profitable, but you get a phenomenal package of benefits for your money.

Triodos Ⓡ Bank

Brunel House, 11 The Promenade, Bristol, BS8 3NN
0500 008 720 (freephone)
www.triodos.co.uk
savings@triodos.co.uk

Organic strength

Eric Schlosser

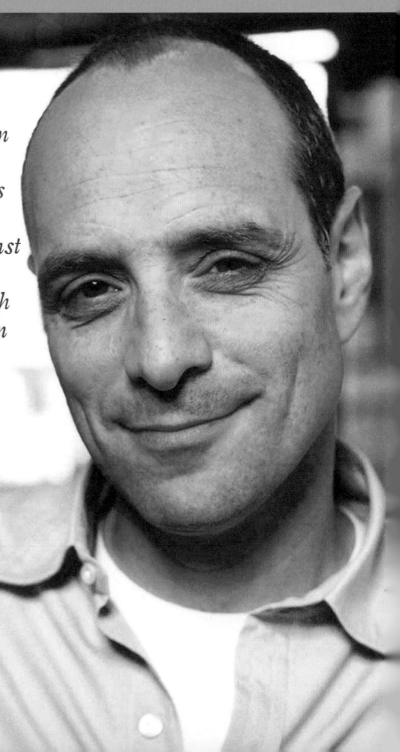

"The economic downturn increased the appeal of cheap foods. But today's well-funded and well-organised attacks against the organic movement are a sign of its strength ... the movement has an invaluable asset on its side: the truth"

🌱 Soil Association

STUFFED*
POSITIVE GLOBAL ACTION TO PREVENT A FOOD CRISIS

Pat Thomas

featuring essays by
Michael Pollan, Geetie Singh, Monty Don, Rob Hopkins, Jeanette Orrey,
Carolyn Steel, Peter Melchett, Vandana Shiva and Eric Schlosser

ecotricity

An extract from Eric Schlosser's essay on the organic movement in Stuffed

"If you believe everything you read in the newspapers, organic food is no healthier than food produced with herbicides and pesticides. In fact, it's 'elitist' – an extravagance for rich people and celebrities – while GM crops are essential to prevent starvation in poor countries people who buy organic food are therefore gullible, trendy, foolish and heartless and it's the multinational chemical companies who care about the poor. It's the agri-business companies who care about protecting the environment. And it's the fast food chains that care about your health. Perhaps we should disband the Soil Association immediately, buy some GM seeds for our gardens and go out for a Big Mac.

The backlash against the organic movement is in full swing, quietly funded and eagerly promoted by the corporations threatened by its success. George Orwell would be impressed by the misinformation. He would have enjoyed the notion that the corporations responsible for today's crises in agriculture, the environment and public health now know the only possible solutions.

The economic downturn increased the appeal of cheap foods. But today's well-funded and well-organised attacks against the organic movement are a sign of its strength. For decades after the founding of the Soil Association, the campaign on behalf of sustainable agriculture was largely ignored. Then it was ridiculed. A quote of Mahatma Gandhi's comes to mind: 'First they ignore you, then they laugh at you, then they fight you, then you win.'

The proponents of industrial agriculture and industrial food spend billions every year promoting their agenda. The marketing budget of the organic movement is insignificant by comparison. But the movement has an invaluable asset on its side: the truth.

The way that we produce food has changed more in the past forty years than in the previous 40,000. And the evidence is conclusive that this industrialised system cannot be sustained. Within forty years it has caused environmental devastation, contaminated rivers and streams and groundwater, spread new forms of infectious diseases, launched epidemics of obesity and diabetes, driven small farmers off the land and imposed terrible cruelties on livestock and low-wage workers. This system is not sustainable, it's incredibly fragile. And without cheap fossil fuels, it will collapse.

Instead of an arrogant and futile effort to control nature, we need to work with it. We need a renewed sense of humility. We were once assured that feeding dead cattle to cattle was a good idea, an efficient use of resources. The lesson to be learned from that fiasco isn't that we all should become Luddites. It's that an industry's short-term desire for profits should never take precedence over a society's long-term survival.

With billions to spend on clever ads, fancy websites and celebrity endorsements, the industrial food system may seem invincible but it is extremely vulnerable. Once people see how this food is made and all the consequences of buying it, they lose their appetite for eating it. They want food that's fresh, local and organic, that's produced without cruelty and without harming the land. And that's precisely why the organic movement is under attack.

Simple changes in personal behaviour can lead to momentous changes. You just have to stop supporting the way that things are. Every purchase is like a vote, an endorsement of the supplier and the thinking behind the product. Refusing to buy food that comes from the industrial system weakens that system. But lasting change will require more than ethical, high-minded shopping. So as long as money dominates politics, multinational corporations will control the politicians. It's incredible that a handful of corporations in the UK now wield more power than its sixty-million citizens. There's no reason that can't change.

When I was born, black and white people in the US couldn't use the same drinking fountains or sleep at the same hotels. I've seen that segregation eliminated, along with the end of apartheid in South Africa, the collapse of the Soviet Union, the fall of the Berlin Wall. These were momentous, systematic changes for the better. And ordinary people made them happen. So when someone tells me that GM crops are inevitable, that factory farms are necessary to produce meat, that we'll always have the Golden Arches, I tell them not to be so sure. Things don't have to be that way, if only enough people want them to be different."

Stuffed, published by Sawday's Fragile Earth, £14.99
www.sawdays.co.uk/bookshop

Go Slow series

published by Alastair Sawday

Go Slow England

'Slow' embraces an appreciation of good food and artisan producers, of craftsmanship and community, landscape and history. In this guide we have a terrific selection of Special Places to Stay owners who offer a counter-balance to our culture of haste and take their time to enjoy life at its most enriching. You will discover an unusual emphasis on inspiring people and will meet farmers, literary people, wine-makers and craftsmen – all rich with stories to tell.

Praise for Go Slow England:

"Go Slow England is our favourite travel book of the year." **Prima**

"Go Slow England is a magnificent guidebook." **BBC Good Food Magazine**

"If you need a break from the rat race, you'll find it here." **Waitrose Food Illustrated**

"If one book sums up what life is like outside England's cities, this is it. It's a homemade-cake-and-jam sort of a book." **Sunday Times Magazine**

"Discover rural idylls, country retreats and slow, slow living as you lie back, stretch out and enjoy the view." **The Guardian**

"This book is a real pleasure and a superb celebration of the best of English life." **The Good Book Guide**

Go Slow Italy

We have handpicked forty-six exceptional places to stay in Italy – birthplace of the Slow movement, home of Slow Food. From the mountainous north, through cypress-dotted Tuscany and on down to the gutsy, colourful south, you will discover owners with an unmatched passion for Slow Food and Slow Travel. Meet farmers, literary people, wine-makers, olive oil producers and craftsmen – all with rich stories to tell. Go Slow Italy celebrates fascinating people, fine architecture, history, landscape and real food.

Praise for Go Slow Italy:

"One of my favourite books of the year." **Amanda Robinson, Editor Italia! Magazine**

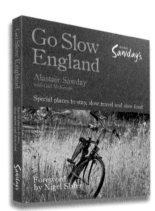

Go Slow
England
UK £19.99
Paperback

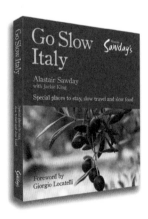

Go Slow Italy
UK £19.99
Paperback

Go Slow France

Living the Slow life comes naturally to the French as they wander down to the boulangerie in the morning for freshly baked baguettes, buy veg, saucissons and bright-eyed fish from their local market or tuck into long and lazy lunches at a family-run restaurant. Let the slower pace of life rub off on you as you explore with Go Slow France.

The range of people and places is pretty amazing: from Alpine chalet to Pyrenean mountain refuge, goat farmers of the May '68 generation to landed gents in their utterly classic family château; a poet with yurts; a single woman running a simple B&B of immense human and cultural interest; a couple of sisters living quietly, organically, in the country and keeping up with all things international to feed the conversation with foreign guests at dinner; a Brit in Provence, whose bones have turned French through love of the place, people, food and wine; artists and historians, a collector of weighing scales, and one of the founders of an early gastropub who left swinging London with his designer wife to bring up a family in saner, healthier climes: the remotest part of central France.

We celebrate the endearing eccentricities of these really special places to stay and the vivacious hospitality of their owners. Visit them and you will drink wine from their own vineyards, eat vegetables from their own potagers and scoff all manner of traditional and oh-so-French cuisine. Bon Voyage!

To order any of these books
Call 01275 395431
or visit our online bookshop
www.sawdays.co.uk/bookshop
for up to 40% discount

Go Slow France
UK £19.99
Paperback

Index

The Welli...
& kid mohair ...
by Simon's Mum